This book is dedicated to Lindsay Cadden.

On The Ball and *Off The Ball* have been a huge success - but a tragedy will always hang over the history of the shows.

After *Off The Ball* on Saturday March 1st 1997 programme producer Lindsay Cadden left to drive to his parents' home in Fife for a family celebration. Tragically, he was killed in a car crash only a few miles from their home. As a mark of respect the show was taken off the air for a week.

Neither Lindsay nor the two presenters he had moulded into something resembling a radio double act would want his death to sadden a comedy football annual. So in the true style of *On the Ball* this book is dedicated to Lindsay Cadden, a dear friend and a big Hibs and East Fife fan.

Ten minutes before he left the studio he borrowed a tenner from Tam and Stuart. And so he died a true Hibs fan – on the scrounge!

First Published by
Greyfriars Press in 1999 a division of Macintosh Red Ltd
19 Hawthornbank Lane, Dean Village, Edinburgh EH4 3BH
Tel: 0131 226 4011 Fax: 0131 225 2671 E-mail: <user>@macred.com ISDN: 0131 226 1186

ISBN 1-903273-00-5

British Library Cataloguing in Publication Data.
A Catalogue for this book is available from the British Library.

Printed by The Belfast University Press, Belfast, Northern Ireland.

Greee

THE RISE AND RISE OF

ON THE BALL

You're tuned to On the Ball – the most petty and ill-informed sports programme on radio…

Every Saturday at 13.05 these self-mocking words introduce a programme that, since its launch in August 1995, has grown into the most successful and highly-rated football entertainment show in the history of Scottish radio…

"…and for the next half hour Scottish football gets annihilated."

On and Off the Ball are listened to in over a quarter of a million Scottish homes each Saturday. That's more people than have passed through Raith Rovers' turnstiles since Elvis Presley was at primary school.

The show is anchored by Radio Scotland's calorific double-act, Stuart Cosgrove and Tam Cowan, a couple of half-baked hypocrites who support St Johnstone and Motherwell respectively. When their teams go head-to-head in the SPL the show bickers on to air, bringing prejudice, acrimony and cheap humour into the nation's homes.

For Cowan, St Johnstone are 'posh' - nothing but a bunch of jumped-up Tory farmers who can barely fill a mini bus. For Cosgrove, Motherwell fans are social degenerates, crawling about in the ruins of Ravenscraig looking for ginger bottles to cash in at the local chippie. The tone has been set – no one is safe. Newspaper stories, injured superstars, high and mighty football administrators are all ritually slaughtered.

Armed with nothing more than cheap gags and bare-faced cheek, the show picks over the rotten corpse of Scottish football. To call the humour sophisticated would be to abuse the English language.

In one of those articles that appear daily in the Scottish press it was rumoured that Rangers were trying to sign the Hamburg goal-keeper George Koch. It was a tailor-made story for *On the Ball*. By the following Saturday Koch jokes were all the rage.

Rangers fans were excited to hear that their new signing was fantastic at corners. He rubbed himself and grew four inches. The theme continued for a week and took a surreal detour when it was rumoured that Rangers were also watching the Croatian internationalist Davor Suker.

Sadly, for the first time in their history, good taste got the better of Rangers - even they couldn't contemplate having Koch and Suker in the same Scottish team.

BOB CRAMPSEY'S BROTHEL CREEPERS

On the Ball's success did not grow in a vacuum. It owes a massive debt to those that came before.

The most obvious influence is the football fanzine culture that grew in the late '70s, and flourished after the punk era. Fanzines like 'When Saturday Comes', Scotland's 'The Absolute Game' and many others produced by groups of fans up and down the country brought an irreverent tone to football, linking supporters' passions to other forms of entertainment like pop music, television and the tabloid press.

Fanzine editors regularly appear on the show and one - Sean Allan of the Hibernian fanzine *Mass Hibsteria* - even agreed to get divorced on the show.

Then there was the trail-blazing success of *Only an Excuse*, which pioneered football comedy on radio, before graduating to television where the formidable comic skills of Jonathan Watson turned the burdz-crazed Frank McAvennie into a modern comic masterpiece.

On the Ball hit the airwaves in August 1995 and soon become a pantomime on air. It has a strain of comedy that goes back to Scottish seaside comedians like Lex Mclean and Andy Cameron, in fact most of Tam Cowan's jokes are so old they were first told at the Gaiety Theatre in Ayr, when Bob Crampsey was a Teddy Boy in brothel creepers.

Tam Cowan is the show's resident comic. He grew up in Lanarkshire in the era of 'alternative comedy' but turned his back on the new comic generation, preferring the 'quick gag' style of older comedians. As a 16 year old schoolboy in Motherwell, he sent jokes into mainstream television comedy shows like Little and Large and Bobby Davro.

Tensions between old and new form the basis of some of the humour. Cowan plays the die-hard Lanarkshire Scot refusing to embrace change, and sneering at the show's e-mail address. Cosgrove by comparison is a modern day media poseur who uses words that his co-presenter claims are "longer than Lorenzo Amoruso's hose-pipe."

Among the show's most popular ingredients are comic staples that have held Scottish humour together for over a hundred years – light-hearted, back-stabbing, low-rent limericks, and short comic sketches, featuring time-honoured characters like grumpy bosses, cheeky cleaners and Glasgow fly-men.

GOODFELLAS...

Much of the creative success of *On The Ball* should be attributed to the script-writers and comic actors who work round the clock to ensure that the show is as topical and biting as it can be when it goes on air on a Saturday lunch-time.

THE VOICES ARE THE INSPIRED WORK OF FORD KIERNAN, LEWIS MACLEOD AND GORDON MUNRO. Between them they can imitate a bewildering array of comic characters, creating the illusion that superstars like Sean Connery, Robbie Coltrane and Billy Connolly are live in the studio.

Over the years, some truly bizarre characters have become audience favourites. The Hearts player Pasquale Bruno was one of the first post-Bosman continentals to play in Scotland. Little is known of Bruno's true personality, but with Ford Kiernan's Joe Pesci style Mafia voice, and script-writers on hand to squeeze any old Godfather gag into the script, it was inevitable that Bruno would become a Mafia hood holding Hearts to ransom. In one memorable sketch Bruno told Tynecastle boss Jim Jefferies to watch his mouth or he would end up with Dave McPherson's head in his bed.

Celtic's Fergus McCann was a gift for the impersonators. His Scots-Canadian drawl and transatlantic affectations made him a real star. Shrewd, mean and scheming he was available every Saturday to clip the wings of big-name signings like Henrik Larsson and Alan Stubbs.

Rangers David Murray was portrayed as a cash-fixated entrepreneur who wanted to turn his back on old values like bigotry and protestant triumphalism, for the New World of debentures, share-issues and revenue streams. But *On the Ball* is yet to be convinced. If Rangers had truly turned their back on bigotry why was everything in their new super-market priced at £16.90?

Another die-hard is the eminent Bob Crampsey, the memory man who holds the history of Scottish football in his head. He appears each week, with the Hovis theme tune playing nostalgically in the background. He knows every detail from the days when Vale of Leven were Scottish Cup holders to the day when his beloved Third Lanark gave up the ghost. Bob Crampsey can remember everything - but he can't remember an edition of the Daily Record that didn't mention Rangers.

CAPPUCCINO & CHIPS

Undoubtedly the characters that fans love the best are Scottish players who are ill at ease with the lifestyles of the rich and famous. Comic portrayals of players like Tosh McKinlay of Celtic and Ian Ferguson of Rangers, are guaranteed a good reaction.

Fergie may have played alongside Paul Gascoigne at Rangers but God ensured he would never appear alongside Bamber Gascoigne on *University Challenge*. Radio fans love his exploits.

It was rumoured on the show that Ferguson once went to an Italian café with his team-mate Sergio Porrini. When they walked in to the Café, Porrini ordered a cappuccino. Asked by the waiter what he fancied, Ferguson replied "Ah'll have a capuccino as well… Ah'm starvin."

As the show gained in popularity, Italian café jokes became a cult among football fans. One night in La Parmigiana in Great Western Road, Charlie Miller couldn't decide what to order. The waiter said "Do you like scampi?" Miller replied. "I like all the Disney films."

To hit all the right notes, the café had to be Italian and the player had to be gifted of foot but not of mind. Tosh McKinlay was in the Santa Lucia in Hamilton with Josef Venglos. The waiter asked if he would care for ginger with his melon. "Naw, said Tosh, the gaffer's ordered wine."

TRULY HONKING

Some of the humour is cuttingly satirical but much of it - in the words of the show - is truly honking. Stuart Cosgrove remembers the day that the phone-in, *Off the Ball*, really took off:

"IT WAS STILL TRYING TO FIND ITS VOICE. Tam and I had only met a few months before. We were stirring things up with a Celtic fan who had rung in to try and convince us that Jackie McNamara should be Scotland's captain. At the time, Celtic were leaking goals. Tam asked the guy to resolve a dilemma – he said he wasn't sure if Celtic's defence were honkin', mingin' or simply bowfin'. So we asked the listeners. The board lit up and the phone lines were jammed. People just caught on. They realised the show was speaking the language of fans. It was bringing Scotland undiluted on to the air, cutting through all the hype that grows up around big money footballers. We were saying the kind of things that Dundee, St Mirren or Raith Rovers fans say every single Saturday. It was as if they all decided at once to get behind the show. After years of listening to pious shite about the old firm, they had a show that spoke for them."

Some callers became stars in their own right. Margaret with the 36DD breasts rings in regularly to challenge young attractive footballers to lay their virginity at the altar of her bedroom. Two Scottish football fans exiled in Norway drove to a hilltop car park to pick up the show. A fan on the Isle of Skye once walked 5 miles to the nearest phone box to phone in. And the Arbroath team rang on a mobile to scoop a prize.

What was the score when Arbroath beat Bon Accord? The answer is 36-0. Although some Bon Accord fans still claim the 18th goal was offside.

eeeeetings!

HIGH SCHOOL CONFIDENTIAL

Some phone-in subjects had a long shelf life. *High School Confidential* invited fans to ring if they were at school with a footballer and *Tradesmen Calling* invited plumbers, electricians and carpet-fitters to ring in if they had ever worked in a footballer's home.

As the historic referendum on devolution gave Scotland its first parliament for 300 years. *On* and *Off the Ball* went from strength to strength. No one could truly claim they were advancing democracy, but they had acquired a unique hold on the nation's trivial obsession with football. A man claimed that Dundee United's Ray McKinnon was once disciplined by a geography teacher for drawing male genitalia on the black-board. A carpet fitter from Fife described Gordon Durie's shag-pile and the problems he had with the under-lay. This was the democracy that Scotland had waited so long to relish.

For the first year of the show's operation the upper echelons of the BBC were concerned that the language of some fans might be too colourful for listeners in the Borders - or indeed defamatory - and they insisted on a internal delay mechanism.

Effectively this meant that if a caller swore live on air, then the producer had an eight second delay to bleep out the offending word before it was transmitted. After a season without significant mishaps and a change in the law governing live phone-in shows, the delay mechanism was abandoned. According to Tam Cowan it was taken to Glasgow Royal Infirmary and was fitted to Stuart Cosgrove's groin. The operation was a success and he can now watch videos of Roddy Grant without too much embarrassment.

WAR ON THE OLD FIRM

One of the reasons for the success of *On The Ball* is its acidic attitude to the Old Firm.

Unlike most other sectors of the Scottish media where Rangers and Celtic get the red carpet treatment, *On the Ball* has a barely disguised contempt for Scotland's big money teams. The show took the calculated gamble that out there in the pubs and clubs of Scotland there were enough people who wanted something different.

A fake news report on the show captured the mood. "Late news just in. Rangers' supremo David Murray is recovering after microsurgery to his posterior. Doctors said there were minor complications, but they have now removed Chick Young's tongue."

Radio Scotland has to appeal to Scottish football fans of every and any persuasion. Even the thousands of Aberdeen fans who've yet to pay their licence fee. The concept of a show aimed above and beyond the Old Firm hype bore fruit by the barrow-load. The idea was helped by the growing number of Old Firm fans who want to distance themselves from the ingrained bigotry of the past and are willing to join the rest of the sane world and laugh at their own teams.

So armed with topical sketches and the events of the previous week *On the Ball* declared war on the Old Firm and the hyped up media coverage that Rangers and Celtic receive from their pals in the Scottish press.

Until the show broke the mould, most football shows in Scotland had been built around the locker-room banter of former professionals. To protect the equilibrium of sectarianism, there was always a Rangers player and a Celtic player.

On The Ball's head-to-head rival in the west of Scotland, Clyde FM's Super Scoreboard, still uses this format today, pitting Rangers' Derek 'Derry' Johnstone against Celtic's David 'Provo' Provan.

On the Ball has turned the old order on its head. Every setback for the Old Firm becomes a perverse victory. It doesn't matter if it's a dodgy result in Europe or a star player caught in bed with a transvestite. *On The Ball* will be back next Saturday to lift the shell protecting Scotland's biggest clubs.

And as if on cue the super-stars of the old firm have given the show a helping hand. Goalkeeper Andy Goram has been an outstanding contributor to the show and in the interests of comedy was generously caught in a four-in-a-bed romp with a teenage girl.

The story had a happy ending – she got six 'o' grades.

Greeeeetings!

In this first *On The Ball* album you'll find our take on all the teams that have been in the Premier league since the show started in 1995.

You'll also come across all the major personalities in the game that we've made fun of down the years such as Fergus McCann, Andy Goram and Gazza.

Another football phenomenon in recent years has been the increasing number of duff foreign imports - the Bosman Balloons - who have swamped Scottish football since the infamous judgement by the European Court. Many are featured in this book.

And there's a large helping of humour from you - the fans - in the form of the best answers supplied for our *Off The Ball* competitions . We realise you'll hate this book - but it's ideal for fixing the table with the wobbly leg.

Tam Cowan   *Stuart Cosgrove*

The Godfarry

" ...a warning against excessive celebrations... **"**

89-99

Jim Farry was never a big fan of the shows. In fact he was one of only two people to threaten *Off the Ball* with legal action. The other was the **cantankerous** football columnist Gerry McNee, the only man in Scotland who has ever jumped out of a window and gone up the way.

The show portrayed Farry as a **meddlesome** bureaucrat, a man more obsessed with the fine detail of rules and regulations than the skills of football. His convoluted language and love of complex legal terms made him a gift to mimics everywhere. Farry would never use a sentence when a paragraph would do. His pronouncements on the game are **legendary.** A red card was never simply a red card it was 'a serious and systemic breach of the most fundamental rules of the game, particularly those pertaining to dissent, as articulated in subsection 2, paragraph iii of the Association's rules and regulations.'

For a decade Farry ruled the SFA headquarters at Park Gardens – the infamous House on the Hill – issuing dictates and dispensing discipline with an iron-rod. He was **Judge Dredd** with a Hitler moustache and footballers and fans alike universally loathed him. But for all his pompousness *On the Ball* had a soft spot for Jim Farry. Maybe it was because he used the committee power of the wee teams to prevent the mighty Old Firm from controlling the game, or maybe it was just a twinkle in his eye. Farry enjoyed playing the villain and behind the dark exterior he liked a laugh.

When things seemed simple Jim Farry would complicate them, especially if it involved the allocation of match tickets. Cash or credit cards were never enough - in Farry's world football fans had to pass **endurance tests** that would have stiffed the Parachute Regiment before they got their hands on a brief.

Farry's greatest moment came in October 1996 in the Estonian capital Tallinn. In one of the most bizarre games in the history of international football, the Scotland team turned up to discover their opponents had **gone missing.** Estonia had refused to travel from their training camp after the kick-off time had been moved forward due to Scotland's complaints about the luminosity of the Estonian floodlights.

On the Ball captured Farry's gathering excitement as it dawned on him that his country was calling. In a game that will be remembered in years to come by the Tartan Army chant "There's Only One **Team in Tallinn,"** Farry's day had come.

Picture a hotel room in a **grubby** Eastern European city. Where other football administrators would have had to kick the champagne bottles beneath the bed and hurriedly send the **Estonian hostess** back to the agency, James Farry's thoughts are of one thing only…*"This is the moment I have been waiting for all my life. My country is calling. At last the outcome of a football match hinges on a memorandum. Craig, call the Tartan Army! Tell them to sing there's only one Jim Farry. The call has come. I must homologate for Scotland!*

The Godfarry ...
89-99

Courtesy - The Sun

> **I seem to have been blamed for everything that's gone wrong in football since the sinking of the TITANIC**

FARRY FACTS#1
Born 1st July 1954. He was brought up in Govanhill area of Glasgow and supported Third Lanark as a boy.

FARRY FACTS#2
"My influences weren't people like JFK or Gandhi they were my parents." Farry's father was a policeman.

FARRY FACTS#3
Schoolboy Farry, an average centre-half, is mistakenly left off the school team sheet… he takes the huff and seeks solace in rugby.

FARRY FACTS#4
In a magazine profile Farry drops his bureaucratic guard and admits he is a fan of Billie Holiday and Miles Davis. But in the humdrum life of Scottish football the nearest he gets to jazz greats is Billy Davis His favourite CD's include Dylan, Vivaldi…and the soundtrack from *Forrest Gump*.

Courtesy - The Sun

Farry preparing to show Gary McAllister **how it's done.**

Competition#1

WHAT WILL JIM FARRY'S NEXT JOB BE?

• **An Islamic. He could then lead the celebrations of Memoramadam.**
(Alan Fraser, Cumbernauld)

• **The Fat Controller in Thomas the Tank Engine.**
(Bryan Thomson, Kirkcaldy)

1989 Jason Donovan and Kylie Minogue are top of the pops and Scotland's under 16 team reach the final of the World Cup. New Chief Executive Jim Farry considers shaving his moustache when he's mistaken for Saudia Arabia's left back.

March '94 Farry builds his reputation as the SFA's top administrator. A fax confirming security arrangements for the Scotland v Holland game is sent to a Glasgow piano shop. Russ Conway dismisses fears of terrorism.

May '94 Farry issues instructions to fans banning excess celebrations at the Scottish Cup final. *The Sun* publishes a front cover of Farry super-imposed with an onion. The headline says - "He's no'a fun yin, he's an onion!"

July '94 Farry bans a charity match between Scotland and Bosnia - on the basis that Scotland defender Colin Calderwood has dispensed enough foreign aid.

June '95 Pina Coladas all round. Farry appoints an SFA think-tank to discuss the future of Scottish football. The panel travels the world looking for inspiration. *On The Ball* retaliates with Hawaiian theme music and secretaries in grass skirts.

7th March '96 Portuguese striker Jorge Cadete, resplendent in a poodle perm, signs for a club that he later claims treated him like a dog. His transfer clearance is received by the SFA - but stays in the in-tray.

17th March '96 Ten days later. Cadete is still in quarantine. His registration is still not cleared by SFA and he is forced to watch a crucial Old Firm match from the stand.

30th March '96 Cadete is finally registered by SFA but the delay has planted the seeds of a bitter feud between Farry's office and Celtic chief Fergus McCann.

1989
'90
'91
'92
'93
'94
'95
'96
'97

The Godfarry
89-99

FARRY FACTS#6

Farry once refused to release clips of Scottish matches to the David Baddiel show Fantasy Football - because it might bring the Scottish game into disrepute! He'd obviously seen the pilot of the series.

FARRY FACTS#5

He once sent a memo to The East of Scotland League informing them of the procedures that must be followed when a trophy is presented. It includes strict details of the official tablecloth! Panic strikes in Penicuik where clean tablecloths are thin on the ground

FARRY FACTS#7

When the game against Belarus was eventually played, half the Tartan Army sang "Farry, Farry get tae f***" and the other half "One Jim Farry…There's only one Jim Farry."

the farry years

1997
J F M A M J J A S O N

1998
J F M A M J J A S O N

1999
J F M A M J J A S O N

Tam's Take...

Let's make one or two things absolutely clear. Jim Farry did not start World War II. Jim Farry was not responsible for the famine in Ethiopia. Jim Farry was not to blame for introducing Ainsley Harriot to our TV screens. And it wasn't Jim Farry who wrote the scripts for Mike and Bernie Winters. But he's been blamed for just about everything else hasn't he? Look up the word 'scapegoat' in the Dictionary of Scottish Football and you'll find a photograph of the former SFA chief.

At one time or other everything from Alan Rough's perm to the price of a pie at Palmerston has apparently been the wee man's fault. What a load of crap. People never seemed to understand that most of the time Farry was merely the public face of the SFA - the man who broke the Park Gardens news to the media. So why did so many people want to shoot Farry when he was only the messenger? Would the same people give the postman an earful if they didn't like their gas bill?

Okay, Farry didn't exactly endear himself to the public with his high and mighty attitude and fondness for talking gobbledegook - it has to be said he often sounded like Stanley Unwin after about forty Rastafarian funny fags. How many times did he tell us there were "insurmountable logistical difficulties" instead of coming clean and admitting the SFA were up shit creek without a paddle?

Even when he got his jotters Farry was unable to tell us he'd be spending his time dabbling in a bit of DIY. His words? "I'm embarking on an extensive home improvements programme." I suppose his £200,000 pay off would have come in handy - after all the wallpaper would have been done in triplicate.

> "How come they never catch **McCoist** trying to get into a boot."

There's a Farry at the bottom of our garden

Courtesy - The Sun

FARRYSPEAK:

> "Except as hereinafter provided in sub para. 10, approval will not be given to the registered player except when the player is a *bona fide* player as stipulated in Section 49 Clause 5 sub section b."

Competition #2

IF JIM FARRY WAS A MOVIE STAR, WHAT WOULD HIS MOST MEMORABLE LINE BE?

Graham Niven of Montrose said he would star in the hard-boiled thriller movie *Dirty Farry*:

> "This is a .44 Fountain pen, the most powerful pen in the world. You're thinking 'did he write five memos or did he write six?' Well in all the excitement I lost count. Do you feel lucky punk?"

Following his departure from the SFA, On the Ball composed the following tribute: (To the tune of "Auld Lang Syne")

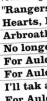

> "Rangers and Celtic I've forgot
> Hearts, Hibs have passed from mind,
> Arbroath, Dundee, Articles two and three,
> No longer interest me.
> For Auld Lang Syne my dears
> For Auld Lang Syne
> I'll tak a memorandum yet
> For Auld Lang Syne

May '97 The Family Final. Farry sends a memo to Cup finalists Kilmarnock and Falkirk warning against excessive celebrations. Both sets of fans jeer Farry as he carries out the pre-match rituals.

1st September '97 Princess Diana dies in car crash. Scotland's match against Belarus coincides with Di's funeral. *On The Ball* backs Farry as the media hound him to cancel the game. The match is on until Rangers trio McCoist, Durie and Goram refuse to play. In a farrago of fake emotionalism, Farry is forced to climb down and the game is rearranged.

4th September '97 The Diana fiasco continues as Farry receives death threats. Media frenzy is at an all time high blaming the French paparazzi, a drunken driver at the Ritz Hotel, and a wee guy from Govan who had nothing to do with it.

March '98 The SFA think tank publishes its report - it is highly critical of the cocktail menu at Sandals in Bermuda and singles the Tequila Sunrise out for serious condemnation.

May '98 Farry calls Goram "a non-person" after the Rangers keeper quits the Scotland World Cup squad training in the USA.

1st March '99 Farry is suspended from duty by the SFA while they investigate the tardy registration of Jorge 'The Poodle' Cadete.

8th March '99 Farry becomes a 'non-person' - sacked by the SFA who buy his silence.

Aberdeen FC

Stereotype FANS

BBC SCOTLAND refuses to sanction references to bestiality on radio but when Aberdeen signed goalie David Preece regular listeners pointed out that his name rhymes with fleece.

'the P45's'

Greatest Contribution to On The Ball

ABERDEEN'S GREATEST CONTRIBUTION to On the Ball was undoubtedly their hilarious start to the season. For the first time in the club's illustrious history former manager and chip shop entrepreneur Willie Miller asked the players to stay away from Harry Ramsden's when they were out on the batter.

Tam's Take...

WHY DO ABERDEEN FANS HATE RANGERS so much when it was Oldham that sold them Paul Bernard? At least I know why Derek McInnes turned his back on four thousand a week - he wanted to play to bigger crowds than that.

In late September '99 after the worst start to a season in the club's history there was great excitement on the Torry Aberdeen supporters bus when the 50p 'first goal sweep- stake' went into an incredible eighth roll-over week. The jackpot stood at £3.50. Two weeks later - the 2nd October - was an even bigger day in the club's history but the Aberdeen players had mixed feelings about clinching their first point of the season against Hibs. They were delighted at breaking their duck but disappointed to discover that the white fivers in the bonus kitty were no longer legal tender.

Although *On The Ball* often has a dig at his wig I'd like to salute Stewart Milne, undoubtedly Scotland's top property developer. The houses he's built are easy to spot - just look out for the ones with the thatched roofs. And this was also the season that a celebrity Aberdeen fan was first spotted in the Dick Donald stand wearing his "Free Derek Whyte" tee shirt.

I'm sure that die-hard Aberdeen fans will want to stay at Pittodrie. But I can't help feeling they'll start the season in new surroundings - the First Division.

Who are you calling a stuffed donkey? At least I haven't been punted by Coventry!

en

❝...a pub team in Malta dispute the rating...❞

FAVOURITE MEDIA CLICHÉ
Aberdeen are the 'sleeping giants' of Scottish football.

CELEBRITY FANS
Richard Gordon and Rob McLean from Sportscene claim they are Aberdeen fans, despite the fact their contracts with the BBC strictly state that supporting anyone other than Rangers is a sackable offence.

FAVOURITE EXCUSE
There's no crisis. We look good in training. We just have to be patient and the results will come.

GREATEST SCANDAL
Sacking a succession of managers when it's obvious the team is just crap....and paying £400,000 for Ilian Kiriakov.

FASHION DISASTER
The hairdos and hairdon'ts.
Big Roy Aitken once tinted his hair purple to get rid of the grey and On the Ball wickedly revealed that chairman Stewart Milne has three wigs. He changes them regularly to delude the world into thinking that rugs can grow.

FORMER 'GER
Derek McInnes paid the Ibrox Club an undisclosed sum not to send him to Pittodrie and, surprise surprise, Eoin Jess was a junior Teddy Bear.

CELTIC DAFT PLAYERS
Derek Whyte is obviously Celtic daft - he gifts them six goals a season.

BIGGEST DUD
Nigel Pepper - who was signed from Bradford reserves. But it may be an optical illusion. He is playing in Aberdeen's worst team ever and may just be finding his level.

UNLUCKY SCOT
Come on...the Scotland team isn't that bad.

TEAM TO HATE
The media try to whip up animosity with Rangers, digging up Neil Simpson's tackle, Ian Durrant's sore leg and the day Andy Cameron got banjoed by a Dons fan. But these days Aberdeen fans hate Aberdeen.

BOSMAN BALLOONS
Celtic fans were delighted when Harald Ingoldsson signed for the Dons. It proved there was more than one Viking balloon called Harald. But some On the Ball fans point the finger at the former Olympiakos striker Taki Hairdous who, reputedly introduced Grecian 2000 to the Pittodrie dressing room in 1995.

WORST RESULT OF THE 90's
The 90's.

COMMENTATORS NIGHTMARE
WINDASS...but that could happen to anybody.

CLUB SONG
'Hey, Hey, MacLeod - Get Off o' Ma Ewe'.

CLUB COLOURS
Red jerseys, **Red** faces.

---

history

1881 Eight teachers were among the twelve men who formed the original 'Aberdeen' team. In 1889 they took over a piece of ground where the Aberdeen Police Mounted Branch deposited their dung. Pittodrie was born.

1903 A true 'don' from Aberdeen University chairs the meeting at which Aberdeen F.C. are founded. The club nominates Eoin Jess's grandfather as the club's first ball boy and say one day he will mature into a great player.

1947 Aberdeen win their first major honour - the Scottish Cup. In a lab at Robert Gordon's College Prof. Herbert Rugg invents a device to conceal male pattern baldness.

1982-84 The high point in Aberdeen's history - the Fergie years. Having won the Scottish Cup in '82 and '83 they went on to beat Real Madrid 2-1 to lift the Cup Winner's Cup...then Hamburg 2-0 in the European Super Cup...and ended season '83-84 as League Champions. Willie Miller builds a chip shop empire from the proceeds.

1990 Alex Smith is manager. Under him Aberdeen win the League Cup and the Scottish Cup. But that's not good enough and they sack him, establishing the club's greatest tradition - the P45.

1992 Aberdeen legend Willie Miller becomes manager. They win hee-haw. P45.

1995 Celtic legend, ex-captain and internationalist Roy Aitken becomes manager. Aberdeen win the Coca-Cola Cup in his first season but the bubble bursts. P45.

1997 Alex Miller becomes manager. He is involved in a boardroom misunderstanding with Chairman Stewart Milne. He thought Milne said "Will you give me herpes?" when in fact he had simply asked "Will you give me the hairpiece?" P45.

1998 Paul Hegarty becomes manager. In a thrifty Aberdonian gesture the club send him a contract stapled to a P45 thus saving the cost of another postage stamp.

1999 Ebbe Skovdahl becomes manager. Aberdeen lose first five games of the season and are rated 473rd in Europe. A pub team in Malta dispute the rating.

1880 1890 1900 1910 20'S 30'S 40'S 50'S 60'S 70'S 80'S 90'S 2000

The Gazza

PAUL GASCOIGNE is one of the most notorious players ever to play in Scottish football. The man-child superstar - signed from Italian club Lazio - became a legend with Rangers fans and manna from heaven for On The Ball. Easily led by his team-mates and followed north by his old pal Jimmy 'Five Bellies' Gardiner, Gazza's exploits have gone down in folk history.

To curry favour with Rangers die-hards in his first match at Ibrox - a friendly against Steaua Bucharest - Gascoigne mimed playing an Orangeman's flute. It seriously backfired on him and he was demonised in the Press and ever after hounded throughout his controversial stay in Scotland. The search for secret flute players became an obsession with the media. In quick succession Andy Goram, Donald Finlay and John Greig all fell foul of the hidden camera.

On The Ball had an ambiguous attitude to Gascoigne, hating what he represented but relishing his every blunder knowing it made great material for the show. In turn he was portrayed as a dupe, a dunderhead and a dull-brained Geordie confused by the pace of life in modern Scotland. The show often caricatured him as a simpleton paired against the streetwise Glaswegian Durrant and in the "Blondie and Butthead" series of sketches he was easily talked into carrying out ill-fated practical jokes such as setting fire to the Ibrox dressing room or putting sugar in Walter Smith's petrol tank.

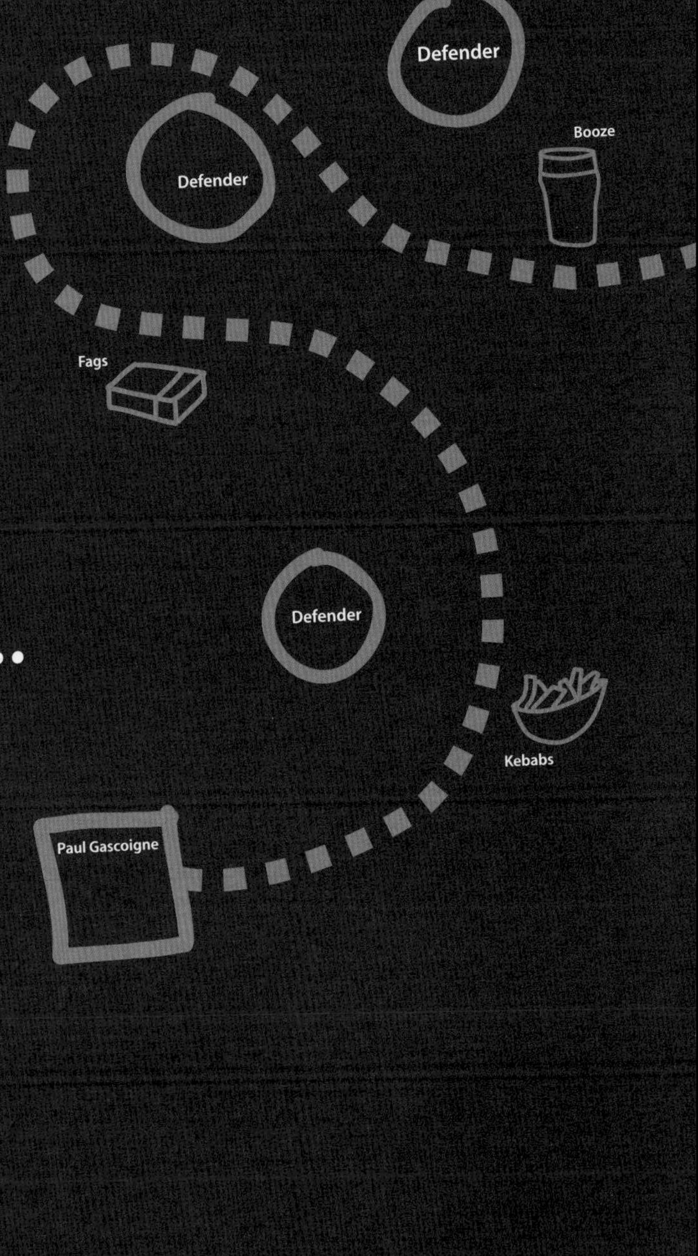

Defender

Booze

Defender

Fags

Years

(bellies galore)...

Defender

Kebabs

Paul Gascoigne

His most trivial and childish moment came not in front of thousands of fans but in the privacy of a Rangers training session when he decided to pee on the Danish internationalist Erik Bo Andersen. But the more the show lampooned Gascoigne the more real life trumped it. He first dyed his hair bleach blonde - a style copied by teenagers throughout Glasgow - and then, to the hairdressers' delight, jet black. He paid thousands for vintage wine in Terence Conran's "Butler's Wharf" restaurant and in an incident that incurred the wrath of the nation he beat up his wife Shezza in the 5 star Gleneagles Hotel. And Tam Cowan took particular delight in the tabloids' revelation that Gascoigne had slept with a 52 year old barmaid, Irene Dunford in the landlady's bedroom above the boozer.

By the time Gascoigne left Rangers only a few untutored fans were sorry to see him go. *On The Ball* hardly missed him. By the time he signed for Middlesborough in March 1998 his antics had become so predictable there was a danger he would bore us all to death. ●

English judge JUSTICE HARMON once famously asked. **'Who is Gazza?'** Perhaps he should have asked, **What is Gazza?**

'What the fox shat?'

The

March '95 A new fashion grips Scotland's worst housing schemes as teenage neds dye their hair peroxide blonde in honour of Rangers' new £4.3m star Paul Gascoigne. Gazza's former club Lazio are glad to see the back of him. A spokesman said "Thank God he's gone - he thought genitalia was an Italian airline."

July '95 James Galway threatens to sue Rangers as Gazza plays an imaginary flute in a friendly against Steaua Bucharest. Rangers fans are disgusted - they thought it should have been a real flute.

Dec '95 During a game against Hibs, referee Douglas Smith drops his cards. Gazza picks them up and 'gives the ref a yellow' Smith books him for his trouble.

Feb '96 Gazza becomes a dad. His wife Sheryl gives birth to Regan. While she is in labour Gazza goes on a bender.

April '96 Voted Scottish Player of the Year. The organisers present him with Dom Perignon. Gazza is delighted - it's the only Mario Puzo novel he's never read.

May '96 Leads a major drinking session to celebrate his 29th birthday while in Hong Kong on England's Far East team tour. The continuing drunken party caused considerable damage to a Cathay Pacific plane bringing the players back home.

June '96 Scores a goal against Scotland at Euro '96, stiffing Rangers' legend Colin Hendry. Ally McCoist ingratiates himself with Question of Sport by rushing to congratulate the English star.

→Newcastle Youth coach Colin Suggett once recommended that Gazza should be released due to his DISRUPTIVE INFLUENCE.

We asked what Gazza's video should be called. The top 5 answers were:

Honey, I've Ignored The Kid
- Robin Grimmond, Dundee

Becks, Lies and Videotape
- Evelyn Smith, Aberdeen

The Tragic Flute
- Scott Bowman, Perth

The Stoned Ranger
- Ian Robertson, Bearsden

The Greatest Toley Ever Sold
- Steve Letford, Connel

COMPETITION

Gazza Years

> **People are gutted...It was like someone had died.**

GAZZA FACTS#1

Academia becomes obsessed with understanding Gazza's personality. Cambridge Professor John Casey described Gazza as 'the weeping, doomed, inarticulate idol of the working classes.' A professor from Strathclyde University is more precise - "He's just a wanker."

GAZZA FACTS#2

Gazza once greeted reporters in Rome by standing up, asking for silence, then farting at ear-splitting volume. When asked for a footballing comment he belched enthusiastically into the mike.

GAZZA FACTS#3

When he met the President of the Danish Football Association, Gazza pretended he could speak Danish by imitating the Swedish chef from The Muppet Show.

Tam's Take...

Gazza once admitted that he cheated on his ex-wife Sheryl... he told her that Rangers would do something in Europe. Actually, talking of Shezza, he never celebrated Christmas Day with her - he always preferred Boxing Day. But he did remember to get presents for his young son Regan. He bought him a jigsaw and nearly amputated his hand when he switched it on. On another occasion he was struggling with a 2000 piece jigsaw of a chicken - Shezza walked in and asked what the hell he was doing with the Cornflakes.

Gazza once refused to speak to the newspapers - as he explained in a two page interview with The Sunday Post. But the biggest back page splash was when he peed on Erik Bo Andersen. This leak may not have been entirely accurate but you know what they say, there's no steam without fire. When in New York Gazza bought a dosser breakfast, lunch and dinner. This didn't surprise me one bit. After the Bo Andersen incident it was clear he enjoyed splashing out on bums.

The O Gazza

ASKED by a Norwegian camera crew if he had a message for England's upcoming opponents Norway he immediately responded **"Yes, F**k off"** then ran away laughing.

Daily Record

Fred West's brother hangs himself

E Coli victims died as list lay under counter

EXCLUSIVE: *Rangers star's Final order*

GAZZA SANK A DOUBLE WHISKY BEFORE KICK-OFF

GAZZA FACTS#4

Jimmy "Five-Bellies" Gardiner was often the butt of Gazza's juvenile sense of humour. Perhaps the foullest of his pranks was when Gazza took the crust off a pie, scooped out the meat and replaced it with cat-shit.

GAZZA FACTS#5

He took a film crew making the documentary about him to a house in Glasgow which he said was his new place. He then pretended he'd forgotten his key and knocked on the door. When a befuddled housewife answered he said he was doing a telly advert and asked if she preferred Daz or Omo.

Years

the Gazza years

J A S O N

1997

J F M A M J J A S O N

1998

J F M A M J J A S O N

1999

J

Oct '96 Gazza goes on drunken rampage at Gleneagles Hotel and beats up his wife Shezza. Womens' groups across Scotland are appalled and a leading feminist claims it's the biggest setback for women since Joan Burnie joined the *Record*.

Oct '96 Sent off against Ajax as Rangers crash out of the Champions League 4-1. Tells press conference "I'm a disgrace."

Nov '96 Gazza drinks a large whisky in the Celtic boardroom moments before the Coca-Cola Cup Final at Parkhead. He burst in wearing full kit, demanded a double and downed it in one as the stunned directors of opponents Hearts watched in disbelief. In the post-match victory bath Rangers players belted out sectarian songs watched by Donald Findlay and John Greig. Afterwards Celtic cleaning ladies refused to clean out the bath. One of the Huns had shat in it.

Nov '97 Ranger Erik Bo Andersen claims that during a training session he felt "something warm" on his back. Gazza is accused of urinating on his Norwegian team-mate.

Feb '98 Gazza has affair with 52 year old ex-model Irene Dunford the only woman in Britain who thinks safe sex is a padded headboard.

March '98 The end of an era. Gazza signs for Middlesborough.

May '98 Gazza destroys his chance of playing for England in the World Cup by going out on the piss, smoking, eating kebabs but most of all by hanging around with Chris Evans.

Players compete in the annual Wim Jansen lookalike competition.

Stereotype FANS

DOES ANYONE KNOW the Latin for pickpockets?

Celtic

'the Bead Rattlers'

Tam's Take...

It gives me no great pleasure to have a pop at Celtic fans. Many of them still haven't recovered from the traumatic years of the mid-90's when they signed 'Yogi' Hughes from Falkirk. The East of Scotland hasn't been been a happy hunting ground for the Hoops. Let's not forget they also signed Darren Jackson - the artist formerly known as mince - who was immediately tagged the worst DJ in Glasgow. Quite a feat considering Clyde FM employs Tiger Tim.

Cynics may suggest I'm anti-Old Firm but to be honest I actually admire some of their players - especially the Scottish internationalists. I was proud of Celtic full back Tosh McKinlay when he went down to Yorkshire TV with Old Firm pal Ian Ferguson to appear on a special edition of Countdown. Channel 4 later confirmed it was the first time the show had ended in a no-score draw.

Also on that special Scottish football edition *Scotland On Sunday* egg-head Graham Spiers appeared in 'Dictionary Corner' and took the honours with a nine letter word in every round - even in the Numbers Game.   Talking of television, remember the launch of Channel 5 when large parts of Scotland couldn't get a decent picture of the Scotland game live from Celtic Park? Not the first time in the '90's there were reports of interference at Parkhead.

Greatest Contribution to On The Ball

SADLY MICHAEL FAGAN'S late-night visit to the Queen's bedroom happened well before the show was invented. So it has to be Fergus. Green Nose Fergus, Fergus the stand-up comic, Fergus the father…and so on. But there was also the night Regi Blinker was done for peeing up a close.

history

1890
1900
1910
20's
30's
40's
50's
60's
70's
80's
90's
2000

AIL! HAIL! HAIL! HAIL!

FASHION DISASTER
STEPHANE MAHE who was deported from France for bad taste after complaints from Paris fashion designers. He was placed in quarantine in Dover before arriving at Parkhead.

"Okay...Okay...if you can't get me John Lambie I'll settle for Murdo McLeod."

ISGOW

❝ ...NOTHING induces sleep quite like the Lisbon Lions... ❞

CLUB COLOURS
Forty shades of **Green** - after only one wash.

FAVOURITE MEDIA CLICHÉ
Nothing induces deep sleep quite like 'The Lisbon Lions'- football's answer to Ovaltine.

GREATEST SCANDAL
Trying to move Celtic to a toxic waste site in Cambuslang...and hiring pop star Michael Jackson to coach Celtic Boys.

FAVOURITE EXCUSE
The referee was once seen on a bus sitting next to a guy whose brother works with an apprentice joiner who comes from Larkhall.

COMMENTATORS NIGHTMARE
Lubomir Moravcik.

FORMER 'GER
C.R. Smith. There is also some doubt about the allegiance of Rangers' Chilean striker Sebastian Rozenthal who arrived from University Cattolica and then claimed he was Jewish. Aye right.

CELTIC DAFT PLAYERS
Mark Burchill made a valiant bid but has always been upstaged by Owen Coyle. The honour goes to Rangers' Giovanni van Bronckhorst who secretly goes to Parkhead to watch his best pal Henrik Larsson.

BIGGEST DUD
Stop if this gets boring...Wayne Biggins, Tony Cascarino, Carl Muggleton, Gary Gillespie...and the commis chef that Lou Macari signed from the Army.

UNLUCKY SCOT
Phil O'Donnell's injury problems tragically prevented him from spending more time on the national team's treatment table.

BOSMAN BALLOONS
The man who single-handedly invented the Norwegian comedy circuit - Harald Brattbakk.

WORST RESULT OF THE 90's
Lost League Cup Final 1994-95 to Raith Rovers on penalties after Paul McStay missed. Gave *On the Ball* the chance to slag them off mercilessly ever since.

CLUB SONG
'Paddy McGinty's Goat.'

1888 In the wake of the Irish potato famine, thousands of hungry Seans come to Scotland looking for a half decent chip shop. Celtic were founded by legendary priest Brother Walfrid in a car park in Barrowfield when he coined the club's motto - "Can I watch yir motor mister?"

1897 Celtic legend Willie Maley appointed as manager. Celtic win Scottish Cup 7 times before World War 1 under his manage- ment. Phil O'Donnell's great-grandfather withdraws from the Battle of the Somme with a pulled hamstring.

1922 Sectarianism first rears its ugly head in Scottish football. Riots break out at the game after Celtic clinch the league title - at Greenock Morton. A Celtic fan throws himself from a crane at Scott Lithgow's shipyard then claims he was going for a pie.

1951 Jock Stein signs for Celtic and plays in the same team as Charlie Tully. The fans pronounce Tully a legend and Stein a dud. Hypocritically this view is reversed by '67.

1953 An internal investigation is ordered when the Croy Celtic Supporters Club complain their bus convener is hiding raffle tickets in his checked bunnet.

1965 Celtic lure Jock Stein back from Dunfermline. They win the Scottish Cup in April '65, then the first of nine league titles in a row in 1966...and then the European Cup in Lisbon in '67 when Inter Milan have an off night.

1972 Celtic beat Ujpest Dozsa 2-1 in Budapest in the European Cup quarter finals. Celtic fans were treated to a post-match champagne and caviar party by Liz Taylor and Richard Burton. A fight breaks out when Burton drinks champagne from a flute.

1983 Charlie Nicholas scores 46 goals in a season but Celtic let him go because he asks for more money. He moves to Arsenal after turning down Liverpool and Spandau Ballet. Frank McAvennie left the club soon after - looking for Charlie. Celtic win the Carfin Chalice.

1991 Liam Brady takes over as manager...followed by Lou Macari...followed by Tommy Burns who they nicked from Kilmarnock. All are hailed as 'Celtic-minded'... then sacked.

1994 The old board is accused of having a "biscuit tin" mentality. Peek Frean threaten to sue. Michael Kelly fails to provide a stadium which meets the requirements of the Taylor Report - or indeed of the 20th century. Celtic bought over by Fergus McCann only 8 minutes before being declared bankrupt.

1998 Glory returns to Paranoia Park. Celtic win their 36th league title and stop Rangers winning ten in a row. Coach Wim Jansen resigns the next day saying he can no longer work with Managing Director Jock Brown.

The McCann YEAR$

(Mr. Magoo)...

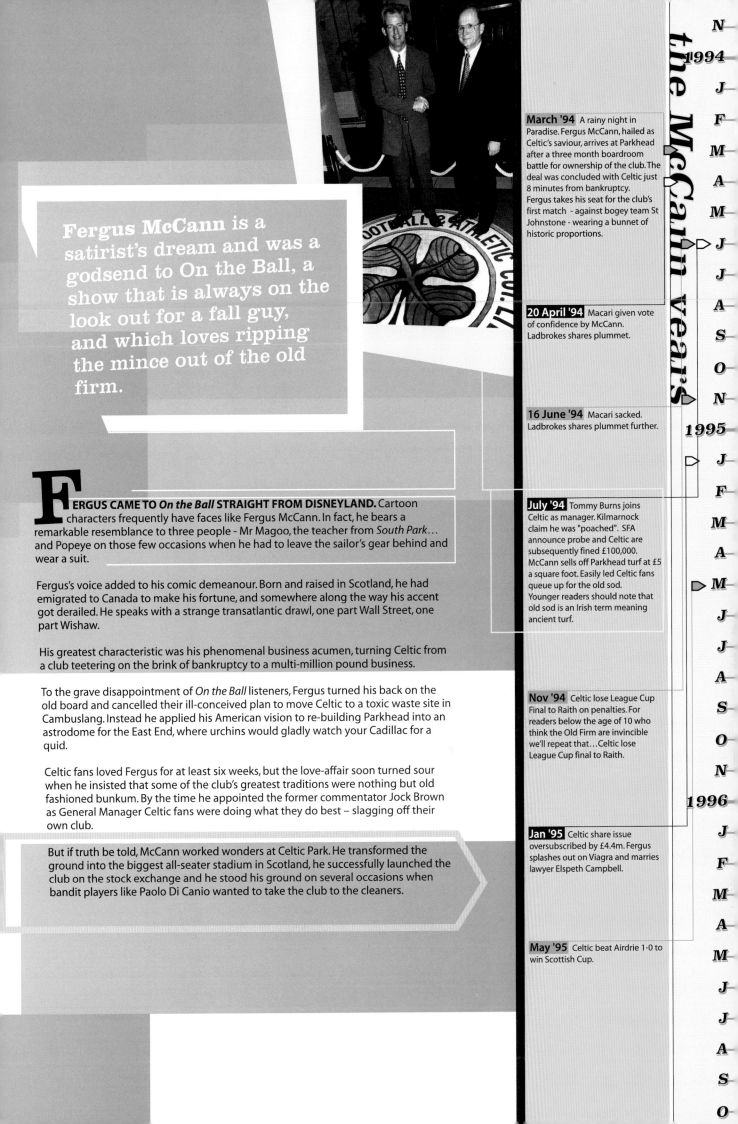

> Fergus McCann is a satirist's dream and was a godsend to On the Ball, a show that is always on the look out for a fall guy, and which loves ripping the mince out of the old firm.

FERGUS CAME TO *On the Ball* STRAIGHT FROM DISNEYLAND. Cartoon characters frequently have faces like Fergus McCann. In fact, he bears a remarkable resemblance to three people - Mr Magoo, the teacher from *South Park*... and Popeye on those few occasions when he had to leave the sailor's gear behind and wear a suit.

Fergus's voice added to his comic demeanour. Born and raised in Scotland, he had emigrated to Canada to make his fortune, and somewhere along the way his accent got derailed. He speaks with a strange transatlantic drawl, one part Wall Street, one part Wishaw.

His greatest characteristic was his phenomenal business acumen, turning Celtic from a club teetering on the brink of bankruptcy to a multi-million pound business.

To the grave disappointment of *On the Ball* listeners, Fergus turned his back on the old board and cancelled their ill-conceived plan to move Celtic to a toxic waste site in Cambuslang. Instead he applied his American vision to re-building Parkhead into an astrodome for the East End, where urchins would gladly watch your Cadillac for a quid.

Celtic fans loved Fergus for at least six weeks, but the love-affair soon turned sour when he insisted that some of the club's greatest traditions were nothing but old fashioned bunkum. By the time he appointed the former commentator Jock Brown as General Manager Celtic fans were doing what they do best – slagging off their own club.

But if truth be told, McCann worked wonders at Celtic Park. He transformed the ground into the biggest all-seater stadium in Scotland, he successfully launched the club on the stock exchange and he stood his ground on several occasions when bandit players like Paolo Di Canio wanted to take the club to the cleaners.

March '94 A rainy night in Paradise. Fergus McCann, hailed as Celtic's saviour, arrives at Parkhead after a three month boardroom battle for ownership of the club. The deal was concluded with Celtic just 8 minutes from bankruptcy. Fergus takes his seat for the club's first match - against bogey team St Johnstone - wearing a bunnet of historic proportions.

20 April '94 Macari given vote of confidence by McCann. Ladbrokes shares plummet.

16 June '94 Macari sacked. Ladbrokes shares plummet further.

July '94 Tommy Burns joins Celtic as manager. Kilmarnock claim he was "poached". SFA announce probe and Celtic are subsequently fined £100,000. McCann sells off Parkhead turf at £5 a square foot. Easily led Celtic fans queue up for the old sod. Younger readers should note that old sod is an Irish term meaning ancient turf.

Nov '94 Celtic lose League Cup Final to Raith on penalties. For readers below the age of 10 who think the Old Firm are invincible we'll repeat that…Celtic lose League Cup final to Raith.

Jan '95 Celtic share issue oversubscribed by £4.4m. Fergus splashes out on Viagra and marries lawyer Elspeth Campbell.

May '95 Celtic beat Airdrie 1-0 to win Scottish Cup.

N 1994
J
F
M
A
M
J
J
A
S
O
N
1995
J
F
M
A
M
J
J
A
S
O
N
1996
J
F
M
A
M
J
J
A
S
O

The McCann YEAR$

"By the way dosser, if there's a rind of bacon in this it's an extra 10p!"

AND - KEEP THIS SECRET - *On the Ball* had a soft spot for Fergus. Anyone who is so universally hated by Rangers and Celtic fans alike must be a good guy deep down.

McCann's exploits were legendary. If there was a half-chance of pulling a fly move Fergus was in there, using either the law or his native cunning to get the best deal for Celtic and - as it later transpired - for himself.

When John Collins moved to Monaco under the Bosman ruling, Fergus cleverly pointed out that he was moving to a principality that was not part of Europe and that Monaco should not benefit from the free movement of labour. He lost but not before he had exhausted every argument on the way to another buck.

Fergus always had his eye on the till. Despite his personal fortune, which now exceeds £50 million, he would argue over a thin dime. Glasgow taxi drivers still tell tales about the day that they picked him up. Every morning he would ring for a cab from his house on the South Side and ask to be taken to Parkhead. **It was always the same friendly greeting...**

Take me to Celtic Park driver. No small talk. And don't deviate from the route.

"It's a Ghirl, not a Bhoy."

Competition#1

BEST CADETE TRANSFER LIMERICK

There once was a guy with a bunnet
Who set out to solve a whodunnit
He registered a player
Then claimed "It's no' fair"
When Jim Farry said "Ah can't fun' it."

(Peter Ottaway, Glasgow)

Oct '95 The Viagra pays off as Fergus becomes a daddy. But the Celtic marketing department is devastated - **it's a ghirl, not a bhoy**.

Jan '96 The famous 'Bhoys Against Bigotry' campaign is launched. The club's supporters renounce bigotry with a rousing chorus of *The Fields of Athenry*.

March '96 Portuguese international Jorge Cadete joins Celtic. Refused clearance by SFA to play in Cup semi-final against Rangers who win 2-1. Fergus blames Farry.

April '96 McCann sends letter of complaint to SFA blaming them for delay in registering Cadete as Celtic player.

June '97 After months of bad press about McCann's Scrooge-like attitude to players, Celtic calm the troubled waters by appointing commentator and lawyer Jock Brown as general manager.

July '97 Wim Jansen takes over as Celtic head coach. Sadly he is a Feyenoord diehard so the old Wim and Ajax jokes fall on stony ground.

Nov '97 Celtic win League Cup beating Dundee Utd 3-0.

9 May '98 Celtic win League title, stopping Rangers from winning the infamous 'ten in a row'.

11 May '98 Victorious coach Wim Jansen quits saying he couldn't work alongside Jock Brown. Crisis at Celtic again.

The McCann YEAR$

Tam's Take...

CELTIC FOOTBALL CLUB was on the verge of bankruptcy when Fergus McCann dipped into his bunnet for the necessary readies and saved the day. But, hey, that doesn't make him a bad person. Always a man for calling a spade a f****** shovel, McCann managed to upset just about everyone during his controversial Parkhead reign. Just ask 'Luigi' Macari, the board of directors at Livingston and poor old Tommy Burns - the Celtic coach who once famously referred to Fergus as "the President."

It was also claimed that he treated Jorge Cadete like a dog though this didn't particularly upset the Portuguese player. He just sat in the dressing room contentedly licking his own bollocks. And Paolo di Canio's penchant for wearing golden boots came about as a direct result of McCann's early years not being particularly successful. As the player later pointed out... "I would have liked silver boots but there was nothing at Parkhead to clean them with."

Fergus was apparently so tight that whenever he sent a suit to the dry cleaners he always stuck a sock in each pocket.

FERGUS FACTS#1
BORN IN STIRLING, he was social secretary of the Croy Celtic Supporters Club. Buses to Celtic away games offered a poor return on revenue so he emigrated to Canada in 1963 to find his fortune.

FERGUS FACTS#2
McCann found his fortune by building up *International Golf* - a company selling Scottish golfing holidays to rich Americans.

FERGUS FACTS#3
In 1995 a special *On The Ball* Christmas Carol commemorated Fergus's visit to a garage where he filled up but made to drive off without flashing the plastic:
"Fuel, fuel the attendant did say,
When you fill up your car you're
obliged to pay"

"It's up to you. You can listen to my version of *Belfast Child* or we'll bring on Jim Kerr again."

July '98 After a long summer search for a new coach, Dr Jo Venglos gives up his job as a lollypop man in Slovakia to come to Celtic. On the opening day of the League when the Championship flag is unfurled the world's most dedicated fans boo McCann's speech.

Aug '98 Celtic crash out of Champions League - beaten 3-0 by Croatia Zagreb in qualifier. Rumours abound that a new dream team want to buy Celtic. U2's Bono and Jim Kerr of Simple Minds are named as investors. Sadly, pop legends Rene and Renata are not interested.

Nov '98 Celtic out of UEFA cup, beaten 4-2 by FC Zurich. Fergus and Jock Brown need a police escort to reach their cars at Glasgow airport. A few days later Jock Brown leaves Celtic. The fans rejoice.

2 Dec '98 Marko Viduka signed from Croatia Zagreb. He immediately insists on dropping the 'o'. The entire Scottish media now call him Mark except *On The Ball* who say it's like calling the famous swordsman 'Zorr'.

5 Dec '98 Viduka walks out on Celtic claiming stress and nervous exhaustion. Three weeks thinking about an excuse that hadn't been used already by Di Canio, Cadete or Van Hooijdonk clearly took its toll.

10 Dec '98 Viduka surfaces in Australia. It's now revealed that the root of his problem is a virus that has gripped Parkhead for decades - money.

Jan '99 Viduka attempts to board the Celtic plane as they head off to Spain for a winter break. Fergus - suffering from air rage - orders him off....but terms are eventually agreed several days later.

March '99 The air rage gets worse as Fergus names former British Aerospace boss Alan McDonald as new Celtic supremo. Delighted that Celtic sacked Jock Brown the Scottish media unanimously decide that McDonald is a great guy.

April '99 Fergus steps down and emigrates to Bermuda counting his forty million - but not before taking the scalp of Jim Farry over the Cadete registration affair.

Competition #2

MARKO VIDUKA LIMERICK

Diagnosed with a nippy verucca
Back to Oz flew young Marko Viduka
He's not right in the head
The bold Fergus said
As he reached for his trusty bazooka

(John Cole)

Dundee FC

'the Bluenoses'

Tam's Take...

ALTHOUGH the Marr brothers have taken over the club and now rule the roost at Dens Park I always had a soft spot for absentee landlord Ron Dixon. He claimed he was a huge fan of Scottish football and a big Dundee supporter - in fact he made a promise to fly in from Canada if Dundee ever reached the final of the Super Bowl.

One week on the show we exclusively revealed that Dundee manager Jim Duffy had been offered a job for life - the club had asked him to track down Mr Dixon. But full respect to the Marrs, they have rebuilt Dens to its current glory and they hope to raise £1m with a share issue - while clubs like Clydebank and Hamilton can only hope to raise £100 with The Big Issue.

Traditionally football fans dislike the board but how can Dundee fans seriously slate Peter Marr. He turned Dens Park into a modern SPL stadium, he turned money over to Jocky Scott to strengthen the squad and he turned a blind eye when Rab Douglas was nicking his daughter.

I'm still amazed how they found the necessary funds to renovate the stadium. Mind you, they did cut corners - there are no baths or showers in the home dressing room. That's Dundee for you.

Greatest Contribution to On The Ball

BALD EX-MANAGER Jim Duffy…and absentee owner Ron Dixon. The Canadian millionaire refused to 'phone the club let alone invest money in the team. For added value he had the same name as the heart-attack Romeo of Brookside and at a time when Dundee's defence took more drugs than Jimmy Corkhill and were about as as fit as Sinbad.

CELEBRITY FANS

Worzel Gummidge and international super criminals everywhere.

Stereotype FANS

There was a break-in at Boots the Chemist in the Nethergate. The thieves took everything but two shelves of deodorant and a jar of brylcreem. Police are looking for a bald Dundee fan.

...Jings, Crivvens, Help Ma Boab...

FAVOURITE MEDIA CLICHÉ
The city that can't support two teams.

GREATEST SCANDAL
When the war in Kosovo was at its height Dundee poured oil on trouble waters by trying to sell shares to international terrorist and Bosnian war bandit Giovanni Di Stefano.

FAVOURITE EXCUSE
If they spent as much on players as they did on the dog track then we wouldn't be in this position.

COMMENTATORS NIGHTMARE
Having to go to Dundee.

FASHION DISASTER
Simon Stainrod's Fedora was the worst hat ever doffed in Scottish football - easily beating Bert Paton's baseball cap and Fergus McCann's bunnet. But even the hat couldn't upstage Simon's shoe. Regular *On The Ball* listeners will recall that this was the shoe Ian McCall dumped in when both were at Falkirk. *What kind of shoes were they?* Brown slip-ons of course.

FORMER 'GER
Eddie Annand…and Steven Boyack once played in the same under-18 team as Barry Ferguson, so he'll never read a paper that doesn't remind him.

CELTIC DAFT PLAYERS
Tommy Coyne is reputedly Celtic daft…but if you base it on crude stereotypes - Irish name and stunted growth - it has to be James Grady.

BIGGEST DUD
Kevin Bain. At 16 he captained the only Scottish team to reach a World Cup final. Sadly, when he grew up, he became Dundee's answer to Colin Calderwood.

BOSMAN BALLOONS
It must be Eric Garcin - and what's more there's no excuse this time. Most Bosman Balloons are bought unseen from some dodgy overseas agent. Garcin was bought from Motherwell - the home of the dud.

TEAM TO HATE
No matter how hard St. Johnstone fans try to wind them up they still hate Dundee United more, much more.

Keeper Rab Douglas gives James Grady a lift home after training.

CLUB COLOURS
Dark Blue with an extremely soiled collar.

WORST RESULT OF THE 90's
Beaten 3-1 by Clyde in the Cup. Even worse it was live on SKY and Charlie Nicholas scored one of the goals - "It wis against the run of play. Dundee threw down the goblet and we were up for it that night - tae be fair."

'The Prince'

CLUB SONG
'We Ain't Got A Barrel Of Money' or the theme to *The Great Escape*.

1893 Two local Dundee teams amalgamate to form 'Dundee FC.' A sound idea. But for years the city was more famous for the three J's - Jam, Jute and Jakeys.

1910 After two drawn games, Dundee beat Clyde 2-1 to win the Scottish Cup. The Sunday Post captures the passion of the game with the headline "Jings, Crivvens, Help Ma Boab."

1938 Dundee relegated for the first time - but not the last. They become one of that select bunch of Scottish teams who see-saw up and down between the top division and the next. Alan Gilzean is born - with hair.

1949 Back in the First Division, Dundee are Championship runners-up. The signing of Billy Steel in 1950 moved them up a gear and 2 consecutive League Cups soon followed. Lucille McLaughlin steals two ration books from a cloakroom at the Caird Hall. Oor Wullie admits he's gay.

1961 Dundee's greatest years were the early sixties. With stars like Gilzean, Ure and Penman they win the League Championship in 1961-62. In '62 they take Europe by storm beating Cologne (8-1), Sporting Lisbon and Anderlecht on the way to the Champions Cup semi-final where they are defeated by eventual winners AC Milan. Reserve player Craig Brown cuts a disc with Hammy and the Hamsters.

1976 Relegated again. Promoted in 1979. Daphne Broon has a lesbian affair.

1980 Relegated again. Promoted in 1981. Paw Broon takes Viagra for the first time.

1990 Relegated again. Promoted in 1992 - the year that Hen Broon successfully undergoes trans-sexual surgery.

1994 Relegated again. Quiet years follow for Dundee, punctuated by the arrival and departure of Simon Stainrod and Jim Duffy as managers…and Ron Dixon as absentee owner.

1997 The wrestler "Prince of Pain" swears revenge on a sneak thief who stole his gear from his car while in Dundee.

1998 Promoted to new Scottish Premier. Confound critics by staying up for season 1999/2000. The 'Dee are back.

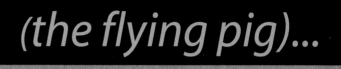

(the flying pig)...

THE GORAM
YEARS

When God made the Goalie he broke the mould. Scandal sticks to ANDY GORAM like a pair of velcro knickers.

No one has given *On the Ball* as much comic material as the former Hibs and Rangers keeper, whose career has sadly gone into free-fall with Lanarkshire Junior side Motherwell.

Whenever the scriptwriters lacked inspiration the lumbering scandal-monger always sprung to mind. Whenever the phone-lines threatened to go quiet Goram was there to take football to new levels of absurdity.

Goram will always be remembered as one of the greatest shot-stoppers in the history of Scottish football, but no matter how spectacular his saves, Andy Goram's on-field exploits were always spectacularly upstaged by his life away from football.

Where do you start? Goram has every weakness known to football. He likes a drink, he likes a punt, his eyes have often strayed to passing skirt and he has some 'friends' in East Belfast.

Although the press have sometimes portrayed Goram as a dark figure who befriends loyalist paramilitaries, *On The Ball* sees him as a cartoon character, more likely to play a cameo role in a Carry On film than anything truly sinister.

Goram's world is a seaside post-card – comprised of caravan romps, bulbous brassieres and bits-on-the-side. His love life would give Mills and Boon a heart attack, his generous contribution to sick animals have been welcomed by bookies throughout Scotland and his escapades up and down the Ayrshire coast would put Casanova to shame.

When Goram walked out on the Scotland world cup squad in 1998 – to try to repair his private life – rumours swept through Scotland that the Goalie was mentally ill. At a league match against Rangers at Ibrox, Kilmarnock's noisy away support diagnosed paranoid schizophrenia, breaking into the now famous terracing anthem – "Two Andy Gorams, there's only two Andy Gorams."

In fact, there are probably five Andy Gorams. The first Andy Goram is the young Lancashire born athlete who was equally gifted at football and simultaneously played in goal for Hibs and as a professional cricketer for Scotland. The second Andy Goram signed for Rangers joining Ally McCoist, Gazza and Ian Durrant in the dressing-room from Hell.

Another Andy Goram is the 'flying pig' - a goalkeeper who defies gravity by throwing his formidable weight through the air to make saves that are truly awesome. A fourth Andy Goram is the one with the dodgy knees. To protect them he had specially designed kneepads made from the same material as wonder-bras.

This trivial fact, irrelevant to many, became a matter of great importance to *On the Ball* listeners who knew from previous programmes that Goram had once had a brief friendship with the abundantly well endowed glamour girl Olga Orbs.

And the fifth Andy Goram is the one who wore a black armband in the wake of the death of the protestant paramilitary Billy Wright. The tabloids claimed it was a sinister display of bigotry, Goram said his auntie in Oldham had died - twelve weeks earlier.

When Andy Goram left Rangers to join Motherwell, logic would tell that he would play out his twilight years in peace, but not so. Within weeks of arriving at Fir Park Goram became embroiled in one of the biggest scandals of his career. An old photograph taken at a supporter's night out showed him posing in front of a UVF banner and all Hell broke loose.

Confronted with the fact that his team's goalie stood accused of bigotry, *On the Ball's* Tam Cowan lamely tried to joke his way out of a corner –

"What's all the fuss about UVF – I don't care what kind of milk he drinks."

Australian fast bowler **Merv Hughes** told Goram '**stick to football**'.

We asked what Andy Goram's pub should be called. The winners were:

The Goalie and Gusset
- C. Downie, Ayr

The Cockwell Inn
- Murray McFayden, Kirkcaldy

The Double Chin and Tonic
- James MacLeod, Currie

The Bird in the Red Hand
- Angus Wallace, Dunfermline

The Shagpile Inn
- Ralph Duval, Helensburgh

(the flying pig)...

THE GORAM YEARS

GORAM FACTS#1

The multi-talented Andy Goram makes his Scotland Cricket debut against Australia in 1989. His first ball is a bouncer from Merv Hughes. Merv tells Goram, 'stick to football.'

GORAM FACTS#2

Goram once bedded porn beauty Louise Montgomery. They made love under a Rangers duvet whilst listening to a Wham CD.

1991 Andy Goram signs for Rangers. A few weeks later Rangers are beaten in the Skol Cup by Hibs courtesy of a Goram slip-up against his old club.

Aug '92 Goram is in a dressing-room punch-up with Nigel Spackman. Says the 'Goalie', "After belting him twice, he went down and curled up on the floor like a hedgehog as I was dragged away."

July '94 Goram is transfer-listed by Rangers. Walter Smith tells Goram it was because he had not made a big enough effort to get fit for the Cup final. Goram's efforts had included a massive bender in Tenerife.

Aug '95 Andy Goram pulls out of the Scotland squad for the game against Finland claiming that he is not mentally attuned. Over the next three years Goram and Leighton would both be in and out of the No. 1 jersey several times.

Nov. '95 Kilmarnock fans show their caring, sensitive side in response to Goram's mental frailty by chanting, 'There's only two Andy Goram's' at a Killie v Rangers game.

Aug. '96 Goram scores with teenage chambermaid Karen Johnston. Their trysting place is a battered old caravan.

Nov. '96 Goram is banned from driving for 18 months plus a £100 fine.

1991
1992
1993
1994
1995
1996
1997

Tam's Take...

Goram was once inspired by Andre Agassi who shaved his torso to be more aerodynamic - Andy tried it and broke the Flymo. He never seemed to have trouble attracting women though and I was always stunned by news of Andy's three-in-a-bed sex sessions - where on earth did they buy a bed big enough?

There was a lot of speculation as to why he quit the Scotland training camp in the States in May 1998. Did he realise that the schools were breaking up for the summer or was he hounded out by President Clinton who was scared Andy would nab all his fly moves? He certainly wasn't himself when he flew back to Scotland. He didn't even ask the stewardess for a look at the black box.

News of Goram's sexual liaisons invariably ended up in the tabloids a few days later. After a fall-out with a Daily Ranger reporter at Ayr Races Andy got back on good terms with the paper after being installed as the favourite to win their new competition - the search for Scotland's Keepie-uppie King.

The Goalie

Goram's self portrait taken from a letter from Andy to Miriam in May '98 while he was in the States.

> ❚❚ If you'd wanted to **sign a runner you should've gone** for **Seb Coe.** ❚❚

GORAM FACTS#3

Andy Goram, 'My Life', the goalkeeper's stunning autobiography is published in 1997. It narrowly fails to win the Booker Prize.

GORAM FACTS#4

In 'My Life' Goram said:
" I honestly believe that the Hibs supporters are the worst supporters in the country."
Goram was subsequently attacked on the pitch at Easter Road by Hibs fan Eric Harvie.

Miriam

GORAM FACTS#5

He also said in 'My Life' that Walter Smith had once given him a hard time during a training run for not being able to keep up with the other players. Goram's reply was "If you'd wanted to sign a runner you should've gone for Seb Coe."

My Face Lights Up With A Dirty Little Smile!

Card to Miriam May '98

Goram with Ex-wife Tracy

Karen Johnston

His "Me + You Kid" x

(the flying pig)...

THE GORAM YEARS

Andy and Miriam today

Look, No Hair!

A HOLE LOT!!

All My Love The Goalie xxxxx

Jan '98 Goram wears black armband in Old Firm game. It is believed to be in memory of murdered UVF terrorist Billy Wright. Goram maintains that it is in memory of his aunt, Lily Scholes, who had died a few months previously. (His own mum doesn't believe him!!!!).

Feb '98 The 'Goalie' breaks Ibrox club rules by letting blonde, Jacqueline Mathieson of 'Laura Ashley' into his Glasgow hotel room hours before a vital game.

May '98 The Scottish Sun exclusively reveals that Goram had a six-month affair with Parkhead sales exec. Janice Dunn. Ms. Dunn claimed that she aborted his baby and that he gave her £900 in used notes for the operation at a Glasgow clinic.

May '98 The portly goalkeeper walks out on the World Cup squad as they prepare for the Finals in France. He makes the decision because of allegations concerning his private life (surprise, surprise!) and his relationship with Ayr barmaid Miriam Wylie.

Jan '99 Goram signs for Motherwell.

Feb '99 Goram's ex-wife tells the Press about his 'den of hate' in the basement of the marital home. It hits the headlines and he is withdrawn from the game against Celtic on 21st February.

August '99 Becomes captain at Motherwell.

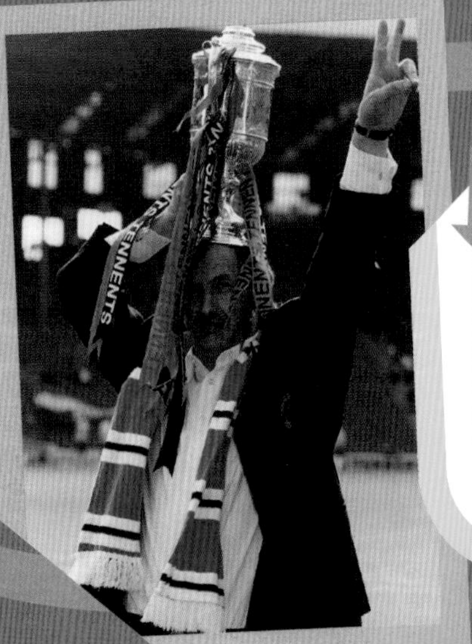

Greatest Contribution to On The Ball

GRUMPY JIM MCLEAN and Ivan Golac's penchant for exotic cigarettes. Also the Saudi nurse Lucille McLaughlin, allegedly a Dundee fan but used to being whipped by the Arabs. But the man who trumped them all was the original ET Davie Dodds who made the front page of the Sun for having sex with a dinner lady. Is that a sausage in your pocket or are you just pleased to see me?

Tam's Take...

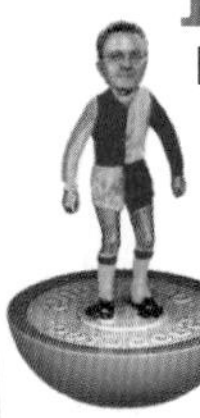

DID YOU KNOW that Tannadice played host to the first beauty contest held in Dundee? - nobody won. Another first is the controversial FIFA proposal to ban tackles in football - it's rumoured they are running a 3 month pilot scheme at Tannadice using Steven Pressley and Brian Welsh as guinea pigs.

United got my creative juices flowing again when they signed… er… um… what's he called again… oh yeah… Quim. It was on the tip of my tongue. Joachim Ferraz - as lily livered commentators insist on calling him - is a rugged striker who has also played at centre half. But United prefer Quim up front as they already have enough cracks in defence.

At the time of writing Quim looks as if he'll do the business at Tannadice but I've only seen him in little snatches. As you'd expect rival Dundee fans have enjoyed taunting the big Portuguese fella - they've really given Quim the sharp end of their tongue. Let's hope no one else rubs him up the wrong way.

CELEBRITY FANS
Lorraine Kelly, Ricky Ross, George Galloway, Yasser Arafat. *On The Ball* fans should also be aware that the BBC reporter Jim Spence was once in a United hooligan gang called the 'Mental Shimmy' and now tries to pretend he's neutral.

Stereotype FANS
Any demeaning Arab reference will do but don't forget they're also from Dundee, so it's two stereotypes for the price of one: *What do you call a bus load of United fans?* - Ali Baba and the Forty Thieves.

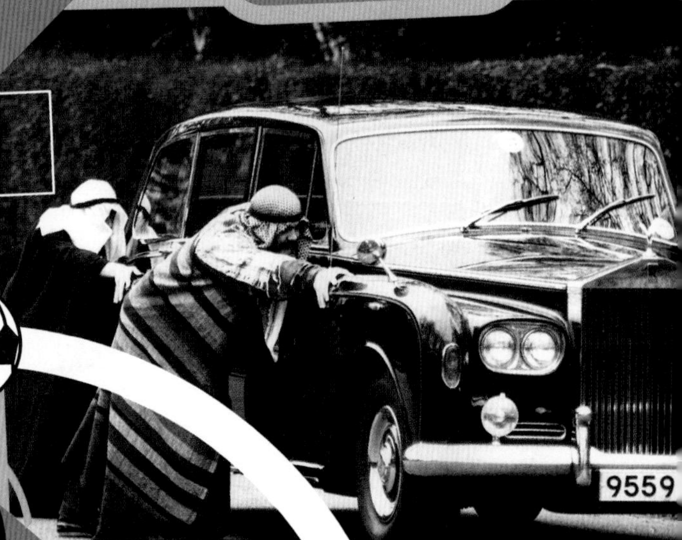

Jim McLean's latest economy drive.

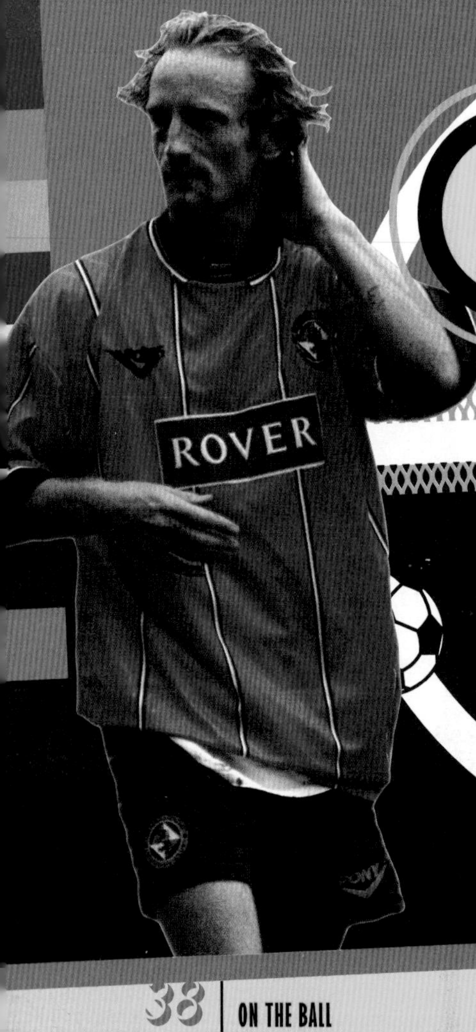

9559

'Tangerine Dreamers'

Dund

ROVER

FASHION DISASTER

Apart from **Sieb Dykstra's** 'porn star' moustache… it has to be striker Raphael Meade who left the club refusing to pay a bill run up at a Dundee department store. The mind truly boggles at the thought of buying your wardrobe from a Dundee department store.

GREATEST SCANDAL

Dave Narey's "toe-poke" against Brazil…and of course they gifted Duncan Ferguson to the world.

FAVOURITE EXCUSE

West coast bias.

COMMENTATORS NIGHTMARE

How to describe a defender getting stuck into Quim without falling foul of the TV watershed.

FORMER 'GER

Stephen Pressley and Gary McSwegan. Fortunately for United they were only passing through.

CELTIC DAFT PLAYERS

On the day of a vital match against the Brendans, former United striker Robbie Winters was actually photographed carrying a 'Who's Who of Celtic' book. Angry fans demanded disciplinary action - although selling him to Aberdeen was a bit harsh.

BIGGEST DUD

A recent poll of Man Utd fans says Ralph Milne but they didn't have to watch the Argentinian guy with the black gloves.

CLUB COLOURS

Tangerine and **Black** with Arafat headgear.

CLUB SONG

'Barcelona, Barcelona what's it like to follow shite?'.

UNLUCKY SCOT

Craig Brewster. He supported them, played for them then did a runner to Greece. If he had signed for Celtic he would still be playing for Scotland now. Spotted by *On The Ball* at the World Cup in France with a gang of other United fans and a three-month old child draped in tartan. Even Herod treated kids better than that.

TEAM TO HATE

Toss up between next door neighbours Dundee or 'new firm' rivals Aberdeen… and don't discount Dundee Junior side St. Joseph's who can afford to spend more in the transfer market.

BOSMAN BALLOONS

United pioneered foreign imports in the 60's with Scandinavians Orjan Persson, Lennart Wing and the splendidly named Finn Dossing. Now there's barely a Scot in the side so take your pick. On the day his wife gave birth, Magnus Skoldmark raced from the maternity ward to Tannadice only to score an own goal.

WORST RESULT OF THE 90's

Sorry, this is a Christmas annual not an encyclopaedia.

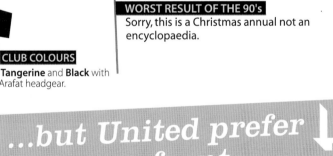

...but United prefer Quim up front...

Dundee UNITED F.C.

TANNADICE - where the laughs never start.

1909 Founded as Dundee Hibernian but by 1923 the club's name falls foul of fan-power when spectators insist it is changed to something marginally less embarrassing like Dundee United. This is the only decision that unites them in 90 years.

1930 The great depression plunges the world into poverty. United lay the ground work for the famous Tannadice academy of excellence. Children from the East End of Glasgow are kidnapped and forced to work night shifts in McLean's jute mills and car wash before being sold to unsuspecting teams in England.

1949 A smile on Jim McLean's face as friends and family gather for his 60th birthday. Maurice Malpas makes his debut against Third Lanark. Deacon Blue's first split.

1959 Dundee United fans embrace the 'new' youth craze - rock 'n' roll which is also, fortuitously, rhyming slang for dole. Maurice Malpas testimonial. Deacon Blue play farewell concert in aid of the legendary full back.

1969 First Summer of Love in Yugoslavia A young Ivan Golac drops his first LSD tab. The hallucinatory effects last for more than twenty years and he is still tripping when he accepts the manager's job at Tannadice. Maurice Malpas testimonial.

1979 Dave Bowman goes to the Odeon in Fintry to see cult movie Alien. On the way out he's stopped for two hours to sign autographs. Another Maurice Malpas testimonial greeted with anger by United fans. Ricky Ross calms them down by announcing that Deacon Blue plan to split.

1983 After forty weeks of following Rangers round Scottish grounds, BBC camera crews suddenly realise United have won the league.

1987 United reach UEFA cup final but lose 2-1 on aggregate to IFK Gothenburg. Deacon Blue record smash hit 'I Feel Dignified In The Rain (You Jammy Swedish Shites)'

1993 Jim Mclean elevated to Chairman. In November he does his bit for Children in Need - he bricks up the boy's gate at Tannadice. Ivan Golac takes over as manager. The club motto is changed to 'Hey, man' and United win the Scottish Cup Final at their 7th attempt in 1994.

1997 Tommy McLean - by amazing co-incidence the brother of Chairman Jim - takes over as manager but they make each other even more depressed. Nepotism reaches new heights a year later when wee Tam is replaced by his brother's secret love child Paul 'Luggy' Sturrock. Ricky Ross becomes reserve team coach.

1999 Maurice Malpas admits he has a bank balance bigger than Prince Rainier's. To celebrate United offer him another testimonial. Deacon Blue re-form and top the bill.

1910
20's
30's
40's
50's
60's
70's
80's
90's
2000

Dearly DEPARTED

HARDLY A WEEK GOES BY IN FOOTBALL without the tabloid back page headlines informing us that some overpriced football property from the Continent or from the Premiership is about to sign for Rangers or Celtic. **The *Daily Ranger* is undoubtedly the worst offender.** If all the signings they have trumpeted over the past few years had come to pass then half of Europe's teams would have passed through the portals of Ibrox stadium. But out of this speculative sensationalism **some have actually signed for the Old Firm.** Here is *On The Ball's* selection of **some of the dudes - and the duds -** who have arrived on and departed the Scottish scene.

Falkirk's Tony Parks can't believe that Oleg Salenko has actually scored.

Salenko & Van Vossen

A queue of highly rated players have mysteriously turned into has-beens on arrival at Ibrox. Oleg Salenko achieved world wide fame when he scored 5 goals for Russia in one World Cup match against Cameroon. He signed for Rangers a year later and repeated the feat by scoring 5 goals in his entire Ibrox career. During his time in Scotland he displayed the kind of movement, co-ordination and accuracy not seen since fellow countryman Boris Yeltsin discovered Blue Label Vodka.

His reputation as a total turkey earned him an appropriate move to Instanbulspor in a swap deal for the tried and tested Dutch internationalist Van Vossen. But it was out of the frying pan and into the industrial strength deep fat fryer when the Van Man arrived. If Van Vossen is remembered for one thing during his time at Ibrox it is being responsible for the most criminal miss since a young Rose West decided she wanted a patio. When Walter Smith was replaced by Dick Advocaat - Van Vossen's former international boss - Advocaat said he could rescue his career. But ten months later he was offered the chance to do something worthwhile for the club - be part of a deal to bring Van Bronckhorst from Feyenoord to Rangers. After being swopped again like a dog-eared Panini sticker he controversially claimed that "Advocaat is wasted at Ibrox." **But it probably lost a lot in the** translation.

Paolo Di Canio

It's always a bad sign when a new Bhoy comes out with the usual tripe about how dear the club is to his heart. Paolo Di Canio honed the bullshit to a fine art. "I always being lifelong fan of the Celtics" he said - and somehow he managed to con Celtic fans that Italian kids kick footballs in the backstreets of Naples dreaming of the day they will play at Parkhead. His £1m move from AC Milan was seen as the best Italian import since Cornettos but within a year it had turned to soor plooms.. Yet again the blame fell on that which is the root of all evil. No, not Fergus - or even Jock. It was money. The emotional Italian was willing to dedicate his future to the club he had always supported as long as they hiked his wages. The reason for the histrionics was merely a grand old scheme to get paid more - eight grand more per week to be precise. To be fair, he did do his bit for the Bhoys Against Bhigotry initiative by turning his back on Celtic paranoia - he claimed that only 90% of referees were out to get him.

He was the highest paid player in the club's history but the tattooed chancer wanted more and he wanted it elsewhere. The fans who'd wanted to shower him with golden boots were now looking to give him the boot with golden showers. The last straw came when he refused to play against Inter Cable Tel in the UEFA Cup although, to be fair, so did the players on the pitch that night. Jock Brown traded him for another golden shower merchant - Regi Blinker. Di Canio's days at Paradise were over and he moved south to join the club he had always dreamed of playing for - Sheffield Wednesday…or is it now West Ham? Dream on Di Canio. Dream on.

❞ I always being lifelong fan of the Celtics !? ❞

Mark Hateley

It seemed that everyone was pleased with Hateley's signing for the Huns in 1995 - the fans, the players but most of all Chick Young. He quickly became a Rangers legend and was also a favourite of the young McCoist as he selflessly laid on a pile of goals, helping 'Super Ally' to win the Golden Boot. Hateley had to be satisfied with winning gold medal at the players' annual fancy dress party. Poor Ian Ferguson - he turned up religiously each year dressed as a pirate only to be upstaged by one of Hateley's Versace jackets.

Hateley's early appearances caught the eye of quite a few interested parties and soon the offers rolled in - Vidal Sassoon, Rita Rusk, in fact anyone with a sharp pair of scissors. Despite a PFA Player of The Year award and a VIP pass to Victoria's his wife told him it was time to move on. Just before he left for QPR his Helensburgh home was burgled and he lost £20,000 of football strips, mementoes and clothes. Hateley's outfits were instantly recognisable and it remains one of the all time criminal mysteries that no-one was caught - "Police are looking for a total pratt wearing a purple jacket with a gold lamé collar." A disappointing time down south was dramatically cut short by a shock return visit to Rangers, the sole purpose being to noise up the Tims in a crucial Old

> **Police are looking for a total pratt wearing a purple jacket with a gold lamé collar.**

Firm match and ensure that Rangers won their nine-in-a-row league title. It worked. He made a big impression on Stewart Kerr's forehead, was red carded then hit the highway to Hull where he offered to take a cut in wages - believed to be the first example of performance related pay in Hull's history and boy, were the performances shocking. Down on his luck there was one place Hateley could still get a gig - Scotland. He threatened to play for St Johnstone… then turned down an offer from Aberdeen (he wasn't that desperate)…and finally turned out for Ross County on a pay by play basis. After a couple of atrocious performances he was sacked and subsequently relegated to a **dream job on Scotsport with Jim Delahunt.**

Jorge Cadete

In 1997 Celtic fans were alarmed to see a permed rocker take the field at Parkhead. Most thought that Def Leppard were playing at the SECC and it was another McCann money making scheme. But Cadete's transfer from Sporting Lisbon is one of Fergus McCann's fondest memories as the player's mysteriously misplaced registration ultimately led to the downfall of McCann's arch enemy - Jim Farry. It soon became clear however that Cadete's psyche was as fragile as Phil O'Donnell's hamstring. The fact that he'd put a "You don't have to be mad to work here but it helps" sticker on his dressing room locker was a bit of a give-away. Who knows what went through that great curly head? Carbon monoxide possibly. Whatever it was, his demands of three times the wages he was getting were outrageous. There was no good explanation - unless of course he had multiple personality disorder and was claiming on behalf of them all. He returned to Portugal for a break, claiming mental illness. Cynics assumed he was lying on a beach in the Algarve but in fact, he'd retreated to a country hideaway where he and his wife run a dog and cat sanctuary. Jorge defended his actions by giving *On The Ball* one of its best ever excuses - Celtic had treated him like a dog. But Jorge has always been kind to animals…after all he's been allowing a poodle to **live on his head for the last ten years.**

Jorge meets new team mate Henrik Larsson

Dear
DEPA

Pierre hitches a lift on Jocky Bjorklund.

What Pierre has under his kilt.

> He had a 'gentleman's agreement' with Fergus McCann guaranteeing increased payments.

Pierre van Hooijdonk

Signed from FC Breda in 1995, Pierre Van Hooijdonk was seen as the answer to Celtic's goal problems - in the absence of buyers for Gordon Marshall, Mark McNally and Malky McKay. It was of course the team that Pierre had always wanted to play for and he hit the ground running with a goal on his debut - then hit the ground sprawling in every game thereafter. He was probably the first foreign player to be cruelly misrepresented by the Dutch press. After that things turned sour and he became furious about his financial position at the club after he learned he had cost less than no-hoper Stuart Slater. His whingeing became so annoying that he was dropped for a 'crucial Old Firm title decider.' His quote the next day that he could "laugh at all the crap at Celtic" showed complete insensitivity towards the Parkhead cleaners who had to pick the solids out of the dressing room jacuzzi after the visit of Rangers.

Van Hooijdonk always claimed he had a 'gentleman's agreement' with Fergus McCann guaranteeing increased payments. But there was nothing in writing and you don't shake the wee man's wallet that easily. Pierre's shameless egocentricity came to light when he moved south to Notts Forest, fell out with his team-mates and was banished from the club. So he will always be cherished for a half decent joke - How many Van Hooijdonks does it take to change a light bulb? One. He just holds the bulb in its socket and **waits for the world to revolve around him.**

Basile Boli

Basile Boli was hailed as the defensive rock that would guarantee Rangers European success. A European Cup medal winner himself with Marseilles, he told the Press that the Ibrox club were good enough to win the Champions' League. Inevitably they printed the story without checking the facts and Basile duly took the field against AEK Athens.

Boli was in fact a true trailblazer with a barrel load of fancy-dan foreign techniques. Although he was slagged off as the original black pudding the truth was he just could not get used to the Rangers training methods - 10 pints of lager every afternoon - and soon fell out with the dressing room because he actually wanted to train. He was possibly the first player in Scotland to conduct a 'misrepresented' interview with the French press when he slagged off Walter Smith's tactics. His boss eventually cleared him when they realised that Inspector Clouseau had turned down the job of translator in favour of former Nantes intellectual Maurice Johnston. More trouble was coming for Bas when Chairman David Murray pointed out that crossing himself when running on to the park was not going down well with the Rangers faithful. Maybe he should have tried something with an imaginary flute instead. Another dodgy French interview later and he was sent packing to a less taxing environment - **Monaco to be exact.**

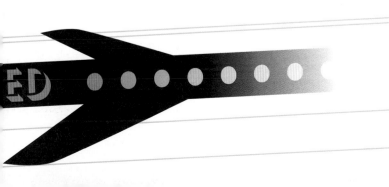

BIGGEST DUD

Andy Smith. No pace, touch or vision but startling talent for dropping his head and blaming others.

Andy does his famous Dumbo impression

FASHION DISASTER

Bert Paton's Headgear. Even Puff Daddy would look a right dick campbell in a black baseball hat and club blazer.

line

...tried to sign Status Quo guitarist Rick Parfitt...

CLUB SONG

Theme from Eastenders.

FAVOURITE MEDIA CLICHÉ

Below Par, Under Par, Par for the Course etc. Sadly, for the Scottish press, Dunfermline have never tried to sign Status Quo guitarist Rick Parfitt.

FAVOURITE EXCUSE

If Jock Stein had stayed they would have won the European Cup.

COMMENTATORS NIGHTMARE

Craig Falconbridge.

GREATEST SCANDAL

The death of captain Norrie McCathie and its complicated aftermath brought Dunfermline to the front page of the tabloids. They also gifted their greatest ever manager, Jock Stein, to Celtic.

FORMER 'GER

Greg Shields and Barry Ferguson's big brother.

CELTIC DAFT

The original - "Celtic daft" Owen Coyle - joined the club in 1999.

UNLUCKY SCOT

Greg Shields -who was a stalwart at the back for the Pars - but now he's moved to the English 1st Division he should be guaranteed a game soon. Incidentally, Dunfermline's most capped player is Istvan Kozma - he has 29 caps for Hungary, 13 of them while he played with Dunfermline.

BOSMAN BALLOONS

Not a balloon himself, but Dutch signing Ivo Den Bieman was so embarrassed by the local balloons in the Pars' dressing room he threatened to change his name by deed poll to Ivo Den Beamer. The real contender would have to be Dunfermline's Brazilian buy Sergio Duarte.

WORST RESULT OF THE 90's

20th March 1999 - Dunfermline 1 St Johnstone 0. Seems like a decent result but it won Dick Campbell the job of manager. Also the Rovers winning the Coca Cola cup.

CLUB COLOURS

Black and **White** - colour transmission hasn't reached Fife yet.

1885 Dunfermline were founded in 1885 when eleven striking miners in Kelty crossed a picket line demanding that Hamish French be sent to the Crimea.

1912-13 Dunfermline are admitted to the Scottish League 2nd Division. At this time the local Press started calling them 'The Pars' because of the parallel lines on their jersey - although some say it was short for 'Paralytics'.

1925-26 Promoted as 2nd Division champions. A young Jim Leishman wins the West Fife Literary Quaich for his celebratory poem.

1927-28 Relegated again as the big Depression sets in...but in Dunfermline it doesn't lift for over thirty years. To bolster their finances the club develop greyhound racing at East End Park which proves more popular than the football.

1960 Jock Stein appointed manager and the Pars win the next six games to avoid relegation. Dunfermline win Scottish Cup for the first time in 1961 - 2-0 over Celtic.

1968 Dunfermline win Scottish Cup again beating Hearts 3-1. In the '68-'69 season they reach the semi finals of the Cup Winners Cup.

1983 People's poet and Panto Dame Jim Leishman arrives to manage Dunfermline. By the time *On The Ball* hits the airwaves Jim is manager of Livingston but still writing poetry. The show called him the man with "all of the rhymes and none of the reason" and often parodied his style:
Red Rum, you were the finest horse
That e'er graced a paddock.
Your grace an' strength beyond compare
Made dolphins look like haddock!

1992-23 The baseball cap era. Bert Paton - a player in the cup winning side of 1968 - becomes manager.

1998-99 The club were on the verge of a take-over deal involving the Japanese club Hyundai United, but not even £8 million worth of government grants could convince the Japs that Gerry Britton was worth 90 minutes. Dick Campbell takes over as manager. His twin Ian is his assistant. Dunfermline are relegated to 1st Division. Dick Campbell resigns in November.

1880
1890
1900
1910
20's
30's
40's
50's
80's
70's
80's
90's
2000

OFF THE BALL

The *Off The Ball* competitions are one of the highlights of the show every Saturday.

Elsewhere in the book you'll find a selection of some of the best answers from a wide selection of fans. We have many regular contributors but on these two pages we'd like to feature the daddy of them all - the guy who's now got more T-shirts than we have - Steve Letford. Hardly a week goes by without a multitude of entries from this man. So - as our most dedicated scribbler we dedicate these pages to him.

Steve Letford

BUT JUST BEFORE WE REPRINT SOME OF STEVE'S HANDIWORK WE THOUGHT WE'D BETTER FIND OUT A BIT ABOUT HIM…AND THIS IS WHAT HE TOLD US.

He was born in 1952 and brought up in Maryhill, a coins throw from Firhill. His brother James took him to his first Thistle game where he found four shillings lying on the ground. After that he was hooked - although it meant the players didn't get a bonus that week either.

Also in those days people took bottles of beer to the game and Steve and the rest of the urchins were allowed to collect them and take them back to the shops to get the deposit. It's a habit he still can't break to this day.

He moved to the West Highlands in 1970 and tried watching shinty instead but he couldn't figure out why the players had the weapons rather than the fans and gave up.

In the early eighties he lived in Holland and played football for an amateur outfit called HRVC where he once had the 'honour' of being kicked up and down the park by Jack Zwaarte the ex-Ajax player who had been in the side that thrashed Liverpool in the famous 'game in the fog.'

And that brings us up to date. Steve and his wife Sheila have two boys called Feargal and Keir and they obviously don't have to buy any tops for them to wear. Steve is presently studying to be a counsellor…but obviously spends too much time writing to us to get to the Diploma!

Competitions

**Jim is White
Jock is Brown
Lex is Gold
And his team's
going down**

Steve's Scribbles...

Things You'll Never Hear in Football:

Jim Delahunt saying "Well, that went without a hitch."
Any Celtic player - "Here, Fergus, you've given me more than I asked for."
"It's Kanchelskis's work rate I admire".
"I miss Gerry McNee".
A coherent sentence from Charlie Nicholas.

Valentine Messages for Football Personalities

Fergus, O Fergus you're growing bolder
But are you looking at me…or over my shoulder?
You've made me a promise that's very exciting
But I think I'd prefer if I had it in writing!

An Aberdeen Goalie called Preece…

**Demanded a wages increase
When told "You've a cheek
After five goals last week"
Said "Leighton would've lost six at least!"**

What Will Happen In Scottish Football In The Year 3000?

Ally McCoist says he'll know when it's time to retire and won't play on past his best.
The Rangers manager says "We've almost got the right blend for Europe and next year could be the one for us".
David Murray posthumously lifts the Ibrox ban on Gerry McNee.

What can be done to stop Hibs running away with the First Division in '98-'99?

They could get the Rangers medical team to look after their players.
Frank McGarvey could put £20 on them to win the division.
The crowd at Hibs matches could be silenced so the players can hear Alex McLeish's instructions.

*POSTIE, POSTIE PLEASE DO HURRY
And take this card to David Murray
A philanthropic man it seems
Who'll do his best for poorer teams
By carving up the TV cash
With those who do not sing The Sash*

*POSTIE, POSTIE DO NOT TARRY
take this card to wee Jim Farry
A bureaucrat with massive powers
Who should've stuck to planting flowers*

Falkirk

'the Badgers'

ESTABLISHED 1876
FALKIRK FOOTBALL CLUB

Tam's Take...

MY FAVOURITE MOMENT watching Falkirk on the box was back in May '97 when they faced Kilmarnock in the 'Family Final.' Who can forget the magical moment when Bairns' boss Alex Totten strolled on to the Ibrox pitch wearing a full dress kilt? Rumour has it that the Falkirk players also wanted to wear the kilt during the match but Totten refused the request saying that there had already been enough loose balls on the park that season. (Fact: according to Bob Crampsey this was the first Scottish Cup Final in history to kick off late). The players were held back while Alex Totten spent 45 minutes admiring the marble staircase.

Any Falkirk fan will tell you that their favourite player in recent years is Kevin 'Crunchie' McAllister - so called because he only changes his Y-fronts once a month. I'm personally disappointed he only won 24 caps for Scotland as he's undoubtedly one of the best Subbuteo players this country has ever produced.

Much as Falkirk fans love McAllister what they won't admit is that infamous Old Firm turncoat Mo Johnston once signed for the Brockville club. There was consternation when he publicly stated he wanted to become Falkirk manager. The bookies were immediately snowed under with bets - on Mojo becoming East Stirling boss later that week. Interesting to know that Falkirk were founded in 1876 - that's exactly 500 years after Brockville was built!

Greatest Contribution to On The Ball

THE INVENTOR OF THE triple-decker pie George Fulston…and one-time manager John Lambie. *On The Ball* portrayed them as a couple of agony uncles who dispensed emotional advice to troubled football personalities. The advice was always the same - **"Cut the Crap".**

Stereotype FANS

IN AN ERA OF ANXIETY about paedophilia it is simply too easy to satirise the Bairns. So *On The Ball* had to invent a stereotype that could be broadcast before the watershed. *Child Line's* Esther Rantzen came to the rescue and Falkirk fans became the 'Esthers.'

UNLUCKY SCOT
Kevin 'Crunchie' McAllister.
One of Scotland's outstanding wingers but lacked the crucial ingredient - he never played for Celtic.

BIGGEST DUD

Six foot seven Kevin James who is now a big dud with Hearts but the most expensive dud was Derek Ferguson who cost Falkirk £325,000 from Sunderland - their biggest ever signing. And Ally Graham.

...Child Line's Esther Rantzen came to the rescue...

FORMER 'GER

David Hagen and Derek Ferguson. 'Del Boy' is still in great demand by idle tabloid hacks as he's the brother of Barry 'Superstar' Ferguson.

CELTIC DAFT PLAYERS

Albert Craig, he always wanted to know the Celtic score...maybe he wanted to know how the rest of his family, Tommy and Jim, were doing.

BOSMAN BALLOONS

Italian waiter and language student Sabatino De Massis.

TEAM TO HATE

Roger Mitchell and Lord Justice Taylor. Also local glamour club Camelon who've been mentioned on Scotsport.

CELEBRITY FANS

Campbell Christie, The Arab Strap and writer Gordon Legge, author of the award winning novel 'Get A Grip Baptie'.

WORST RESULT OF THE 90's

Losing cup semi-final to Hearts in 1998 must rank as the biggest wrench. To this day Falkirk fans can barely believe they lost - to Hearts.

FAVOURITE MEDIA CLICHÉ

A Premier League team in a Second Division stadium.

GREATEST SCANDAL

English import Tony Finnegan. He played one great game for the club, disappeared back down south for a few days on some pretext and sent his younger brother back to Falkirk instead. The brother was dire but it was weeks before anyone noticed the scam. And of course the hole that is Brockville.

FAVOURITE EXCUSE

A Third Division team in a Second Division stadium.

COMMENTATORS NIGHTMARE

Trying to distinguish between Tony Finnegan and his brother was a problem. Jim Delahunt once did a double take when he tried to pronounce the name of Falkirk 'keeper Myles Hogarth. He thought he was presenting the BBC arts show *Omnibus* and the audience - thinking it was a new Gaelic programme - switched off.

FASHION DISASTER

Those minging chequered strips of the **Chris Waddle era** which, incidentally, were designed by George Fulston's daughter.

Rousing half-time entertainment at Brockville.

CLUB SONG

'There's Only One F In Falkirk' although away fans prefer the traditional 'Stand Up If You've Got A Seat'

CLUB COLOURS

Navy Blue or whatever the Fulstons can get a job lot of.

1876 Falkirk founded but it wasn't until East Stirling were established in 1880 that local interest in the game took off. Falkirk's first home game was against Bonnybridge Grass-hoppers. The gate money was three shillings and fourpence. Today's gate receipts at Brockville have more than trebled that amount.

1885 After being itinerant for some years the Bairns return to their first ground - Brockville. The club's official website says that it was "somewhat primitive compared with the stadium of the present day." The mind boggles.

1903 After many years in the 'Scottish Combination' league - which included Rangers and Celtic reserves - Falkirk are admitted to the Scottish League 2nd Division...but are warned that Brockville is a hole and must be improved.

1913 Falkirk win the Scottish Cup for the first time. At the STUC Conference in Dunoon, Chairman Campbell Christie supports an NUR motion which proposes building two railway stations in Falkirk just to confuse away fans.

1953 Falkirk sign Bob Shankly from Glenbuck Cherrypickers. Shankly becomes the pivot of the team which regained promotion to the 1st Division. The popular radio show *On The Batter* invites listeners to compile limericks starting with the line *There was a young man called Shanks...*

1957 Falkirk win Scottish Cup again. On this occasion the final was against Kilmarnock, Falkirk winning 2-1 after a replay. Alex Totten celebrates by saying it's almost as good as walking up the marble staircase at Ibrox.

1976-77 In their Centenary Year Falkirk are relegated to Div. 2. Promoted again in 1980 but they will become one of that select band of Scottish clubs who seem to see-saw endlessly between the top division and the next.

1997 Falkirk are in the Scottish Cup Final once more. This time they go down 1-0 to Killie in what patronising press hacks called "The Family Final."

1998 Any hopes Falkirk have of joining the new SPL are dashed when they are told that Brockville is a hole and doesn't qualify as a stadium fit for the 20th Century never mind the 21st.

1870
1880
1890
1900
1910
20's
30's
40's
50's
60's
70's
80's
90's
2000

Bon Soir Bonnie Scotland

At the World Cup in France '98

Off The Ball was taken on the road. The shows were presented live from cafés, hotels and local bars, reaching record audiences and carrying news of the **tartan army** back to Scotland.

One programme was recorded in a Paris supermarket and featured a truly surreal interview in which a French housewife taught Tam Cowan the best way to suck over-ripe melons. Even

One programme was recorded in a Paris supermarket and featured a truly surreal interview in which a French housewife, taught Tam Cowan the best way to suck over-ripe melons. Even **Benny Hill** would have recoiled at the noises that escaped from the shocked mouth of the well known Motherwell pervert.

The first show was broadcast live from the cellars of the infamous *Auld Alliance* bar in Paris. With the Tartan Army in full voice in the background, fans back home who were packing their bags to make the journey to France were ringing in from all over Scotland.

It was a night that will become legendary in Scottish football. **Ewan McGregor** was serving behind the bar, Fish of Marillion was behaving like a true Hibs fan – stealing drinks from the tables - and actor **Richard Wilson,** famed for his miserly portrayal of Victor Meldrew, made an inspired speech from the top of a table.

The tabloid press flooded to the bar hoping for a big story. And they got one. The failed English internationalist Stan Collymore kicked his girlfriend **Ulrika Jonsson.** and she staggered backwards though the hurriedly arranged lion rampant that separated the *Off The Ball* makeshift studio from the heaving bar.

It was the beginning of three weeks of **staggering backwards** on a trip that would end inevitably with Scotland's defeat.

Broadcasting every night, the show built up a unique relationship with its audience. On the day before Scotland played in the curtain raiser against the mighty Brazil, the show invited callers to shop Scotland's meanest boss. Some companies had let people leave work early. Others had declared an unofficial holiday. But a furniture shop in Edinburgh had insisted its staff work all day and miss the match. The owners were berated nightly on the radio, dubbed Scotland's meanest company and subjected to a barrage of jokes about **Stewart Milne's rug** and Tommy's Carpet Burns.

The shows followed the Tartan Army from Paris to Bordeaux and on to St Etienne capturing the unique essence of Scotland's **doomed voyage** across France. Players were spotted on the way - Hearts captain Gary Locke under the Eiffel Tower and former Dundee United star Craig Brewster - emerging from the draw against Norway with Scotland's youngest fan - a three month old baby. By far the biggest bevvy merchants were Marino Keith's pals and a gang of highlanders led by Duncan Shearer.

The fans crowded into the central square in St Etienne as the *Off the Ball* team were facing a crisis 50 kilometres away in motel-hell on an industrial estate in a dump of a town called Roanne.

In an incident that still baffles health experts Tam Cowan fell ill with food poisoning and couldn't eat for three days. A doctor was called out on the Sunday to inject his corpulent rear end with an antibiotic agent -not the first time a Motherwell fan had felt a prick that season.

Sensing an insurance claim, Cosgrove asked the doctor to record the reason for his visit on the French medical form. The doctor scribbled the words 'Sunday visit' in the appropriate box. Being French he wrote it in French – *'visite du dimanche',* and being a doctor he was only willing to scribble a short abbreviation – VD. Needless to say, Cowan never claimed on his insurance when the tattered show returned to Scotland.

With a hiding from Morocco still fresh in their memory, the show invited fans to console the nation with renditions of *Flower of Scotland* - preferably to be played on household objects. Patriotism was sky high as an air-freshener, cheese graters, cans of Export and half empty wine glasses played out a sad lament for Craig Brown's bravehearts - creamed by the only team we thought we would beat. It was the same old story - *bon soir* Bonnie Scotland - you were never in the hunt.

World Cup '98
DIARY

Tam and Steve Hollywood
(Producer)

Sat 6/06/98

• Depart Glasgow - Fly to Paris.

• Arrive in Paris in a thunderstorm. Paris is in the grip of a public transport strike, taxis are very rare. Stuart cuts a deal with a crazy hairy Turkish guy (who claims to be a taxi driver) - the deal is we give him 200f (£20) we give **him** directions and in return he doesn't drive to some god forsaken Parisian 'burb mug us, rape us and kebab us. On the way into Paris our driver advises Stuart that smoking cigars and snorting a little cocaine (just a little) will make you a great success with "les femmes"; drinking Cognac on the other hand will make your cock shrivel to the size of his fat hairy little pinky. Despite the fact that we've agreed the money up front he takes us the scenic route and about an hour later we arrive at our hotel - the charming, family run "Hotel Massenet."

• Head off to get registration from FIFA media headquarters - unfortunately we're registered as "Angleterre" - Stuart kicks up an almighty stink (to no avail). Tam however sees advantages- "Now we can go around starting fights and the **British** media will just blame the French police - although, being English, does this mean we now have to find Ainsley Harriot funny?"

• Night time- head out to sample the best that French cuisine has to offer - big disappointment.

Sunday 7/06/98

• Spend the day exploring Paris - **bateaux mouche** trip along the Seine (Stuart tries to push Tam in - "That would be **in-Seine**" -the boat is called the Edith Piaf -("Pee-aff - I thought that was a command"). See Left Bank , Pompidiou Centre etc.....

• Search is on for Scottish newspapers - however there is no Record or Evening Times (not even a Dundee Courier). Tam's French is so bad that he "reluctantly" has to make do with "mags that only have pictures in them"

• Tam and Stuart head off to the supermarket for some refreshments - however being a Motherwell and St Johnstone fan they are bewildered by this "Champagne" stuff.

• Stuart fancies some Chateauneuf Du Pape "That's the castle of the nine papes - aye wait till Jock Brown sorts that out." Tam starts yanking a chicken around - "Well it said **poulet!**" He's also on the search for some really, **really** strong detergent -"C'mon Stuart - how was I to know what a bidet was for". It takes an eternity to get served 'cause the tills are mobbed with guys from Aberdeen with bags of empty ginger bottles.

Mon 8/06/98

• Auld Alliance Bar for the first programme - the place is absolutely mobbed and you can hardly hear yourself think. Stuart opens the prog -"Bonsoir, Bonsoir there's a dug in my car." Tam - "Frankly I'm disappointed, I didn't come all the way to France to spend the evening playing darts with guys from Bo'ness".

• Dr Cosgrove implores the nation to call in so he can dish out sick lines for tomorrow afternoon - John from Edinburgh calls in to shop his boss who is refusing to shut his furniture shop - "What does it matter you're only armchair fans anyway."

• Hamish calls to say he's just leaving for Paris from Ayr. Tam - "If you're leaving from Ayr then you're going the right way."

• The big game is 2 days away but reports are coming through that there are already 1000 "foot soldiers" of the Tartan Army staying at a camp-site in the Bois de Boulogne - "Although there is also a butch site for us real men" adds Tam.

• The England Squad is out-doing Scotland on the scandal front - Gazza is thrown out of the squad for being drunk and Teddy Sheringham is alleged to have spent a drunken half hour in a toilet cubicle with a karaoke singer - worse news still, as reports filter through that Billy McKinlay has taken his acoustic guitar to the camp with him "to help boost morale."

• Auld Alliance - Ewan McGregor, Ally McCoist, Ulrika Johnson and Stan Collymore arrive - Collymore falls out with Ulrikaka and ends up kicking her on the floor. Tam - "we heard Ulrika Jonsson was getting physical with a footballer - but that's hardly news is it?"

• We spend a pleasant evening in a street side café on the Rue de Rivoli boozing and schmoozing.

• Stuart out on the bevvy with mates from Perth.

Stuart and Tam and mates before Scotland v Brazil - France '98

ON THE BALL

World Cup '98
DIARY

Tues 9/06/98

• Stuart wakes up - sounds like shit, and has half a Parisian bus shelter in his room.

• Rubbing shoulders with other journos down at the media centre we speak to Radio 4 commentator Alan Green - only realise he's not English after he manages to speak for two and a half minutes without mentioning 1966.

• Do the evening programme from BBC Sport offices overlooking the Seine and The Eiffel Tower - the street below the window is teeming with Tartan Army (as is the whole of Paris). Expectation is reaching fever pitch. Stuart predicts "it's either going to be 1-0 or 5-0 - basically I can't see Brazil scoring", Tam has been to the spanking new Stade De France and saw the Brazilian squad training. Ronaldo is panicking he asks Tam "Can you show me a few of John Philliben's free kick tricks. Apparently Ronaldo speaks broken English as he always comes over to see his relatives in Wishaw every New Year.

• Julie from East Kilbride calls in to complain that she has to work during the game - she works in her **husbands** window cleaning business and the rotten bugger won't give her the afternoon off. She does however offer to support Scotland by walking under her ladder in a Brazil top whilst the game is on. She also passes on top window cleaning tip - always use a really, really dry shammy to avoid smears (entertaining and informative thus fulfilling our public service remit.)

• Valerie- a dentist from Arden- pleads with her patients not to have toothache after 3 pm tomorrow.

• That night Paris grinds to a standstill as the interminably dull opening ceremony cavalcade lumbers it's way through the streets (two giant robots) - fans are so bored they start noising up the gendarmes. There's a wee bit of a riot - the Scottish fans are sort of involved but the blame is eventually laid at the feet of the Argentian "Barra Bravas" a 300 strong gang of hardcore nutters who've come all the way over from South America for a bit of aggro.

Wed 10/06/98 SCOTLAND 1 Brazil 2; (Morocco 2 Norway 2)

• Set off for the game - Tam in specially made tartan suit, Stuart in tartan Shirt (Stuart's mate Tam gets cheap ticket just as game starts). Tam meets Alex Ferguson -"That's some suit you're wearin' son." Tam replies "I hope Jim Leighton has a great game just to get it right up you". Atmosphere is better outside the ground than in. Inside it's just loads of media types and freeloaders. Tam - "It was a bit like a reserve match - you could hear the players shoutin' to each other". Cesar Sampaio scores from a corner in 4 mins - he then brings down Gallacher before half time and Collins scores from the penalty. Tom Boyd nets an own goal, Brazil win - but the nation knows we wiz robbed. Tam also sneaks a peek at Pele's cock in the toilets at half time.

• First late night phone in - Stuart has lost his voice, both sound near suicidal - "Welcome to Radio Scotland's late night Samaritan service". Gordon calls in and cheers them up by playing Flower of Scotland on a musical box; David calls up from Skye after walking 5 miles to phone box; Irene confesses she gets so nervous during Scotland games that she listens to the radio with the volume turned down! Tam- "Em..Irene, have you been at the super lager?"

Thursday 11/06/98 Italy 2 Chile 2; Austria 1 Cameroon 1

• A day for reflection. We seek out two mathematical geniuses, Jerome and Benjamin, to see what Scotland's chances for progress are after yesterday's results. Something gets lost in the translation "trigonometry and calculus - did you know Paula Yates has had twins?" "Fractions speak louder than words."

• Back down at the FIFA media centre we bump into top Italian journo Jacobi Savali (the Jim Traynor of Milan.) Once again something is lost in the translation, as he informs us that Amoruso, Porrini and Negri are all highly rated in Italy. "So do they feature in the Italian squad?" "No". Even **Gattuso** is highly rated in Italy, and Jacobi gets a little terse when Tam inquires as to how the Italian U21 captain got through Italian Quarantine -"They must be very lax". So what does he think of Duncan Ferguson? - "Matto" - "What does 'matto' mean?" - "It means crazee"

Morton Fans invade the studio - Bordeaux

Friday 12/06/98 Saudia Arabia 0 Denmark 1; France 3 South America 0

• Oops - too much sun, vin and baguettes goes to our head as we ask the nation to nominate which English celebrity they would most like to give a good kicking (apart from Stan Collymore) A ten year old from Aberdeen calls in to say he'd like to kick the living crap out of Alan Shearer. Switch boards are jammed, letters are sent to MP's and we're reported to the Broadcasting Standards Commission.

• The French at last get into the spirit of things as France win their first match 3-0 against South Africa - the fans take to the streets and we're trapped in a taxi on the Rue di Rivoli by thousands of cheering, flag wielding fans.

Saturday 13/06/98 Nigeria 2 Spain 3; Holland 0 Belgium 0; South Korea 1 Mexico 3

• Paris is invaded by Belgian and Dutch Fans - the Champs Elysees turns orange as the Dutch take over. Stuart tries his chances with some burds from the Netherlands - they turn out to be three Ajax supporting blokes dressed up as fish wives. Tam is more impressed by the South Korean fans who've taught him a new song:

**I've grilled a wild rover for many a year
and a wee Yorkshire terrier is great with a beer
I do not eat Corgi cos I'm not a yuppie
just give me a hot dog and a medium slush puppy**

Sunday 14/06/98 Yugoslavia 1 Iran 0; Argentina 1 Japan 0; Jamaica 1 Croatia 3

• Transfer day - Paris to Bordeaux by plane. When we arrive in Bordeaux the Tartan Army are already there in strength. We're staying at the Hotel IBIS in the centre of town - which is mobbed with drunken Scottish scumbags and the Norwegian FA. Meanwhile in Marseilles the English fans go on the rampage. The atmos in Bordeaux couldn't be more different - it's the start of a 3 day party. Tam and Stuart are mobbed in the street by fans demanding photos and autographs - they must have mistaken them for celebrities or something.

Monday 15/06/98 Germany 2 USA 0; England 2 Tunisia 0; Romania 1 Colombia 0

• Meet up with local fashion journalist Linda Cordada from the Bordelaise style mag *Stylo et Ecran*. Tam and Stuart ask her why they've had so little success with "le talent" as they've been round the Pigalle - Tam -"I thought is was pronounced Pig-alley" They want to know where she gets all her trendy gear - "At **What every French Woman Wants?**"

• We do the prog back at the hotel with a live audience - a posse of Morton fans from Greenock - Tam -"Bet this is the biggest crowd you've been in for years." They sing us out of the prog with a rousing chorus of "We'd walk a thousand miles for one of your goals - Scoooawwwwottttttland!"

• English fans are rioting in Marseille (again). We instead reflect upon the Danish "Rolligans." These sickeningly cute Scandinavians aim to be the antithesis of the hooligans - they wear stupid red clap hats, most of them have beards and they claim to come in peace - Tam -"Come in piece - that's it I'm not having any more of those baguettes, and there was me thinking it was just mayonnaise."

• Find a curry house - "Best meal I've had since we got here" - Tam.

• The kindly producer lends his bed to a destitute Scots family, the darling children repay the favour by peeing the bed.

Tues 16/06/98 SCOTLAND 1 Norway 1; Brazil 3 Morocco 0

• Best day of the competition - walk to the ground with the rest of the Scotland fans.

• Some Norwegian guy scores but we equalise through Craig Burley. Christian Dailly spends the whole day skinning Vidar Riseth on the left wing but never once gets a decent cross into the box.

• After the show, back at the hotel, Stuart enjoys an eightsome reel with Colin Hendry's mum while Jackie McNamara's dad is giving the Gay Gordons laldy.

• We ask callers to call in with their renditions of Flower of Scotland. Ian (the drummer from the Fir Park Club "you name any tune and he can ruin it") plays it on his teeth; Keith and Aileen from Lockerbie do it with a Peach and Jasmine flavoured Haze 2-in-1, a cheese grater and a spoon..."that was rotten but I bet your living room smells lovely now"); Peter in a fishing boat in the North Sea plays it on his foghorn ..."that's great Peter but I bet the guys in the boat next to you are now playing it in his underpants"; Michael from Edinburgh plays it on half empty wine bottles - his "bevy-phonium"...Tam -"you sound like an Aberdonian going to the shops with all his ginger bottles." Biggest controversy of the campaign as Tam and Stuart disagree violently as to who was the winner.

MARDI 16 JUIN 1998 A 17H30
ECOSSE / NORVEGE
TRIBUNE
TRIB. FACE HAUT VERT
ACCES   RANG   PLACE
MEDIAS   32   115
MATCH
17
FRANCE 98
COUPE DU MONDE

...the darling children repay the favour by peeing the bed.

The On the Ball hi-tech studio for France '98!

Friday 19/06/98 Nigeria 1 Bulgaria 0; Spain 0 Paraguay 0 (the most boring game - ever)

• Stuart is still in London.
???????????????????

Saturday 20/06/98 Belgium 2 Mexico 2; Holland 5 South Korea 0

• Tam spends the whole day out and about in Paris - the sun is scorching but Tam insists "I'm fae Lanarkshire - I don't need sunscreen".

Sunday 21/06/98 Germany 2 Yugoslavia 2; USA 1 Iran 2; Argentina 5 Jamaica 0

• Spend the day travelling down to St Etienne. Nice TGV to Lyon (the train is full of Iran and USA fans) then a sweaty cattle truck to St Etienne - Tam is feeling like shit and sweating like a dog. When we arrive in St Etienne the taxi driver laughs insanely and rubs his hands with glee when we tell him where we want to go - Roanne is 50km from St Etienne and the taxi costs a ga-zillion Francs. Unfortunately we're not even staying in Roanne - we're staying in an industrial estate near(ish) Roanne called Meriadeck...in "motel hell".
• No programme today cos Tam is far too sick.
• Call out doctor - VD (visite du Dimanche) etc....

Wed 17/06/98 Chile 1 Austria 1; Italy 3 Cameroon 0

• Transfer day - back to Paris and the hotel Massenet. Stuart promptly poofs off back to UK cos he's got some gayboy Channel 4 work to do - Tam and producer Steve (the hard guys) stay and tough it out.

Thursday 18/06/98 South Africa 1 Denmark 1; France 4 Saudi Arabia 0

• Stuart is still in London.
• It's unbelievably hot in Paris and we're staying in a hotel without any air conditioning - Tam hasn't slept for days and is looking for a remedy, luckily.....
• Huge story breaks - Craig Brown made a record in 1964 when he was with Dundee, "My dream came true" by Hammy and the Hamsters, featuring Hundee cohorts Alex Hamilton, Kenny Cameron, Alex Stuart and Hugh Robertson. We play the record on the prog and Tam's sleep problem is solved. He dubs it "The worst managerial record since Roy Aitken at Aberdeen"
• Once again Paris goes Tonto mental as France beat Saudi Arabia 4-0

Tuesday 23/06/98 SCOTLAND 0
Morocco 3; Norway 2 Brazil 1

• Tam goes to the game in his tartan night gown (if I remember rightly).

• Take a taxi for the 50km trip to St Etienne (that's a 100 km round trip)

• 3-0 doing. End of a team (Calderwood, Boyd etc surely they'll never kick another ball for Scotland?) Tartan Army stands and applauds for half an hour after the game.

• Post match phone in: "Reality bites… and reality bit Scotland well and truly on the bottom tonight." Tam consoles Stuart, he reminds us we're returning to a land of plenty - "square sausage, curries, Harry Ramsden's, real bread - no' this crusty baguette stuff".

• Jill calls in from Dundee to tell us her son's car has been stolen and trashed while he's in France - "how am I going to tell him?" "Don't worry if he's in the tartan army he'll probably stand and applaud the thieves for half an hour". John calls in from 'the Peoples Republic' of East Kilbride to point out that Scotland have just jumped from 44th in the Fifa ranking to 32nd (i.e. the worst team out of the 32 teams in the World Cup) -"If this news is relayed to the stadium in St Etienne the fans'll probably stay there 'till 2006."

• Once again we're asking for renditions of Flower of Scotland - Jim calls in, he gives it a go on a can of export (the one can he drank when the game was still interesting) and buttons off the telly - Tam - "Jim, see when you're on the bus do you lick the windows?" Caroline tries her hand with half filled glasses of water - Tam -"seven glasses filled with water - takes me back to that New Year party up in Aberdeen last year"…while Scott and his wife Debbie fail to get the point of the whole exercise and play it on a keyboard! We end the programme as Tam joins Marianne gargling a slow and mournful rendition of Flower of Scotland. Stuart- "All you die-hards, all you night owls, it's only football, it's only the game we love. Cry not, fear not for tomorrow there are bacon rolls to feed our hungry nation.

It's all over I'm afraid - **bon soir** Bonnie Scotland"

《fin》

ON THE BALL

World Cup'98
DIARY

Monday 22/06/98 Colombia 1 Tunisia 0; Romania 2 England 1

• Tam is still ill - we do the prog with Richard Gordon. Big talking point - where is Craig Burley going to play - through the middle or wide on the right?

• Worth remembering at this point that we all really believed Scotland were going to beat Morocco and we were busy making preparations for the next round, looking forward to our next destination - St Remy in Provence - where the rest of the BBC and the Scotland team were camped in luxury for most of the trip.

• After the prog we watch Romania beating England with Richard Gordon, Rob MacLean, Chick Young and David Begg - Chick and Richard wind up the English guests by going mental when Romania score a late winner. After game we head off to the bright lights of Roanne…not.

HEARTS WIN
SCOTTISH CUP
for the 6th time in
their history beating
the mighty Rangers in
the final...

Heart OF

'the Pacemakers'

H M F C

Greatest Contribution to On The Ball

ITALIAN STALLION Pasquale Bruno was one of the first high profile Italians in Scottish football. The show portrayed him as a Mafia Don, who told Jim Jefferies if he didn't pick him, he'd wake up with Dave McPherson's head in his bed.

Tam's Take...

YOU CAN'T BEAT HEARTS when it comes to buying players. Hans Eskillsson and Justin Fashanu in one season - what a result! Former English internationalist Fashanu was delighted to join the Tynecastle club although the smile disappeared later that season when FIFA banned the tackle from behind. Fash had already been the Queen of Diamonds and was later tipped to join Kilmarnock - but decided against the move as the stripes made him look fat.

Hearts Chairman Chris Robinson's trait of being economical with the truth didn't start in 1999 - a couple of seasons earlier he claimed that Hans Eskillsson was a striker. Eskillsson looked like a refugee from the Hair Bear Bunch and played football like one too. His jaw-dropping performances in front of goal eventually raised suspicions amongst his team-mates that something was amiss. Before training one morning three of them dragged him into the changing room, took a pair of shears to his hair...and unearthed Tony Cascarino.

Hearts No. 1 fan Stephen Hendry - my arse - once said he would emigrate if Labour won the election in 1997 - apparently the Shadow Chancellor had plans to put £4.50 on a bottle of Clearasil. In season 1998-99 Hearts often reduced their fans to tears - but I still reach for the Kleenex whenever I think of Neil Berry's testimonial. After 13 years at the club he only played 10 minutes before being stretchered off. What a crying shame. Imagine spending 13 years with Hearts.

Stereotype FANS

IT WOULD BE TOO EASY to call them the Edinburgh Huns so *On the Ball* favours the Jam Tarts.

FART of MIDLOTHIAN

idlothian

"...will be forever associated with diptheria..."

FAVOURITE MEDIA CLICHÉ

Having blown the league on the last day twice they are 'The Nearly Men' - even their fanzine is called Always the Bridesmaid.

GREATEST SCANDAL

Wallace Mercer's hostile bid to buy Hibs preceded *On the Ball* but fortunately Hearts' Christmas party in Newcastle is always good for few fights and they at least had the decency to sign a French guy that had been done for drugs.

FAVOURITE EXCUSE

When the club were at war with the Daily Record and withdrew co-operation it lent credence to an age old Edinburgh excuse - west coast media bias.

COMMENTATORS NIGHTMARE

Jose Quitongo. Getting his name right is always tricky. Catching him diving is easy.

CELEBRITY FANS

SNP leader Alex Salmond and Edinburgh Provost Eric Milligan are Tynecastle's political vanguard. But Hearts' biggest celebrity fan is snooker star Stephen Hendry. Some say he spends more time playing golf at Gleneagles or going to Ibrox with David Murray to be a real Hearts fan. But *On the Ball* is convinced he's a true Jambo - his complexion is a dead give away and his wife's maiden name is Tartt.

FORMER 'GER

Dave McPherson, Derek Ferguson, Stephen Pressley, Gary McSwegan, Sandy Clark, Tommy McLean. In fact lawyers at the European Court of Human Rights are analysing contract law to see if former Rangers players are obliged to go to Tynecastle or if there is a get out clause.

WORST RESULT OF THE 90's

Humped 6-0 by Falkirk at Brockville, a result that would be rank in any decade never mind the '90s.

BIGGEST DUD

Stefane Salvatori was a border-line Bosman Balloon until he met Stuart Cosgrove in a café in Rose Street and said how much he loved *On the Ball*. He was let off the hook. Mind you, the Italian was never a serious contender not at a club who had signed a Frenchman called Stephane Paille. On his arrival Hearts fans thought his name was pronounced PAIL - and he liked a bucket. Alas it was pronounced PIE and he was forever mince.

UNLUCKY SCOT

Scott Crabbe was someone who showed real promise and was touted for a Scotland cap. But he broke his leg and is now with Falkirk, which doesn't entirely rule him out, but it should.

BOSMAN BALLOONS

Hans Eskilsson and Stephan Paille.

TEAM TO HATE

Obviously the Hibees. At the height of Edinburgh's AIDS epidemic Jambos nick-named them the H.I.Vs. They also have a grudging hatred for Kilmarnock who beat them on the last day of the 1965 season to clinch the League.

CLUB COLOURS

Hearts club colours are traditionally maroon which is a relief to limerick writers. It's the only colour that rhymes with Hen Broon, big balloon and goin' doon.

FASHION DISASTER

Dave McPherson's hairstyles have charmed Scottish football across the decades. He once had a mullett longer than Ozzy Ozbourne.

CLUB SONG

Every time they bottle it listen for the gentle sounds of Blondie's *Heart of Glass*.

1874 Hearts are founded. Historians think that the club take their name from Walter Scott's famous Waverley novel *Heart of Midlothian*. But the name actually came from a dance hall on the Royal Mile. Unfortunately the Slug and Lettuce didn't open for another 120 years or they might have had an even more romantic name.

1886 Hearts settle at Tynecastle Park in Edinburgh's Gorgie Road - an address that will be forever associated with diptheria and dire Wednesday night matches.

1890 Hearts are the only club from the far East to be founder members of the Scottish League. The following year they win the Scottish Cup. Fans naively think this is the shape of things to come.

1914 The entire playing staff go off to fight in the trenches. They suffer from severe shell-shock at the Battle of the Somme and don't recover until the 1950's.

1956 Hearts win Scottish Cup for 4th time. The late 50's was a golden era for the club with stars such as 'Tiger' Dave MacKay, Jimmy Wardhaugh and Willie Bauld, whose name alone alerted the CSA to suspect that he might be Chick Young's dad. They are League Champions in '58 and '60 and win the League Cup 4 times in this period. Another star of the era is Alfie Conn Sr, whose son goes on to defy logic by playing for Rangers and Celtic.

1976 It's the year of punk and Hearts fans scream, wail and spit as the Jambos are relegated. For a few years they pretend they are Dunfermline, getting promoted and relegated with monotonous regularity.

1983 Viagra is invented in a pharmaceutical laboratory in the USA. Samples are stolen and find their way on to the Edinburgh black market. Hearts are promoted to Premier and somehow manage to stay up.

1993 Tommy McLean takes over as manager but he is only there as a tourist and a Stagecoach bus is parked outside waiting to take him on to Kirkcaldy and Dundee.

1998 Hearts win Scottish Cup for the sixth time in their history beating Rangers in the final. Manager Jim Jefferies finally has proof of West coast media bias -the result is mysteriously missing from Glasgow football bible The Wee Red Book.

1870
1880
1890
1900
1910
20's
30's
40's
50's
60's
70's
80's
90's
2000

The Sex Files

"THE ELEPHANT MAN"

DAVIE DODDS AND THE DINNER LADY

Davie Dodds and wife Jill.

AN UNMISTAKEABLE FACE was spotted leaving a council flat in one of Dundee's earthier neighbourhoods in the early hours of the morning of 30th August 1996. It was the flat of Dundee school dinner lady Jackie Webster... assured of her place in the history of Scottish football philandering for having had a year long affair with Davie Dodds.

DAVIE WAS ALREADY WELL KNOWN to *On The Ball* fans as E.T. - one of the world's least glamorous males and a man who will never give Leonardo di Caprio a sleepless night. The show made a point of congratulating the school involved for giving a blind person such an important post.

AT THAT TIME Davie's coaching role at Ibrox took him all round the country to check out local talent - and even to watch some footballers as well. His wife Jill eventually became suspicious after thousands of pounds were mysteriously withdrawn from their bank account - a sum Davie dismissed as gambling debts. In fairness, he had been going to the dogs for a while.

BUT YOU ALSO HAVE TO WONDER about Jackie's state of mind and ask if she had been exposed to some BSE infected beef in the school canteen.

THE MORAL OF THE STORY though is - never underestimate the power of food. If the way to a man's heart is through his stomach, Davie was probably hooked from the minute he tasted her pies.

HUGH WARD - THE SHAGGING POSTIE

POSTMAN HUGH

Postman Hugh,
Postman Hugh,
beds your wife then
hides in the loo.
Early in the morning,
When her man's out
working,
Pops around and
empties out his sack.

Postman Hugh,
Postman Hugh,
he got caught now
he's black and blue,
That'll teach him a
lesson,
Now there'll be no
messin',
What a red neck -
playing for
Dumbarton!

The *Record* headline of April 23rd 1997 just about said it all:

"I belted Striker for scoring with my wife."

POOR POSTMAN HUGH. The part-time Dumbarton striker must have thought he'd landed a sure fire scoring method when he met 35 year old Jenny Falconer on his rounds in Helensburgh.

SHE'D RECENTLY SPLIT from her civil servant husband Kenny and after a hard morning Hugh liked nothing better than to empty his sac at her place. It's not known why she was so keen on him although as a Dumbarton player it should be pointed out he had lots of experience in going down.

BUT THE COURSE OF TRUE LUST never ran smoothly. Just as Hugh was enjoying a mouthful one lunchtime who should appear unexpectedly but husband Kenny. He said "When Jenny came to the door she had nothing on but a t-shirt. It was lunchtime and she would normally have been dressed. She was acting strangely and I knew something was going on." Falconer found Postman Hugh hiding - crouched naked behind the toilet door - and gave him two black eyes for his trouble.

CRAIG HIGNETT-COCK OF THE NORTH

IN MARCH 1998, just before he signed for Aberdeen from Middlesborough, Craig Hignett was accused by his wife of having an affair with Tees-side TV presenter Judie McCourt.

JUDIE WAS NO ORDINARY 'B' LIST CELEB - she was the former girlfriend of samba superstar Juninho so perhaps young Craig relished the chance to test his ball skills against those of the Brazilian star. Anyway, Hignett angrily denied her accusations but was quizzed by cops after his wife - who has a black belt in karate - alleged he gave her a black eye to go with it.

JUST WHEN IT SEEMED things couldn't get any worse he got a phone call from Alex Miller asking him to come and play for Aberdeen - and that was his next mistake.

THE PRICK FROM PERTH

FOLLOWING A SCOTTISH CUP semi-final in 1999 in which his beloved St Johnstone crashed to a 4-0 defeat at the hands of Rangers, a certain Stuart Cosgrove was given his marching orders by Strathclyde Police.

APPARENTLY said Mr Cosgrove was behaving in a loudmouthed manner (surely not!) in Glasgow's Queen Street Station where he was seeing some pals on to the last train to Perth after an evening drowning their sorrows.

WHEN MEDIA MOGUL COSGROVE began to give a rendition of *Have You Seen a Handsome Hun …No…No* the Strathclyde Constabulary became somewhat alarmed. The cops warned him to stop immediately or face arrest. And with a voice like his WHO CAN BLAME THEM?

The Sex Files

R OWAN ALEXANDER made his name as a striker with Morton and St Mirren - hence the "Super Ro" -and has had a lifelong love of football.

BUT BACK IN JANUARY 1999, while he was Queen of the South gaffer, his wife decided he was seeing too much of the Queens. She gave him the ultimatum "It's football or me." There was no contest. Alexander set up the sofa bed inside his office at Palmerston and settled down to a life of floodlit dinners for one.

HOWEVER, his relationship with the club soon hit a sticky patch and he found himself out on his ear there too. On the rebound, he signed for Cumnock Juniors who play in Division One of the 'Stagecoach Western League.' Quite a come down for the man who once played against Cruyff and Gullit while in UEFA Cup action for St Mirren.

BUT *On The Ball* stuck with Rowan through thick and thin. He will always be remembered as a man of principle. During his nine year spell with Morton he always refused to leave his Dumfriesshire pig farm to move north to Greenock. And who can blame him.

RO, RO SUPER RO-ROWAN ALEXANDER

Hibs players model Barry Lavety's new jersey.

Stereotype FANS

An extra from TRAINSPOTTING whose mother runs a sauna in Leith.

Hibern

'the HIV's'

Tam's Take...

THE ONLY GROUND where the match commentator insists on putting a condom over the microphone, Easter Road has provided the show with a wealth of material. For example, did you know that Hibs inspired a FIFA plan to curb time wasting and make the game flow more easily - they issued Scottish referees with yellow cards that have Willie Miller's name already printed on them.

Barry Lavety was another Hibs player that kept the show going. Although he didn't enjoy the best of times at Easter Road the greatest disappoinment of his life centred around a football stadium 500 miles to the south - he was too young to travel with the tartan army to Wembley in 1977 and missed out on the opportunity to return with loads of grass.

Another source of amusement was the Hibs stage show featuring Russell Hunter and Una Maclean - Scotland's answer to Tom Cruise and Nicole Kidman. It was an absolute belter of a production and, in keeping with club tradition, the audience left with twenty minutes still to go.

Hibs have always been a charitable club. They gave George Best a game when he was down on his luck, they rescued Grant Brebner from Tommy Burns's Reading and in 1997 they did their bit for Help The Aged by paying a weekly wage to 64 year old Ray Wilkins.

Greatest Contribution to On The Ball

To the tune of Spandau Ballet's *"Gold - you're indestructible"* Edinburgh businessman Lex Gold appeared frequently on *On The Ball* trying to sell the SPL to the nation. Meanwhile Hibs were doing what they do best - getting relegated.

"It's bad enough being in the *Ku Klux Klan* without expecting me to support Hibs, Mr. Farmer."

GREATEST SCANDAL
Being relegated in '98...and that purple away strip.

CELTIC DAFT PLAYERS
Pat McGinlay - who thinks he's still playing for them.

an

⇓⇓ **...visionary training methods - cider and LSD...** ⇓⇓

CLUB SONG
'My Father's A Lavvy Attendant' or 'In Your Tynecastle Slums.'

FAVOURITE MEDIA CLICHÉ
The Famous Five. They trip off every football fan's lips - Smith, Johnstone, Turnbull… Ormond …and that other one.

FAVOURITE EXCUSE
Tom Farmer - he's got deep pockets but surprisingly short arms.

COMMENTATORS NIGHTMARE
Ollie Gotskalksson who helped Hibs get relegated to Division 1 allowing *On The Ball* to dig out the Proclaimers' old number *Cap In Hand* featuring the lyrics "I don't know why Stranraer lie so lowly, they could save a lot of points by signing Hibs goalie".
Dream on.

FASHION DISASTER
The white tape which covers Dirk Lehmann's ear-rings. Even the fans started wearing them.

FORMER 'GER
Alex Miller. Always Alex Miller.

BIGGEST DUD
Joe Tortolano is one of the ultimate duds in the history of Scottish football. Manager Jim Duffy came a close second. The bald Duffy arrived at Hibs in a helicopter during the Edinburgh Festival - the nearest he's been to a fringe in ten years.

UNLUCKY SCOT
Kevin 'Crunchie' McAllister is probably the most unlucky Scot in the history of the professional game. If ever a guy deserved a Scottish cap it was 'Crunchie'. (See Falkirk.)

BOSMAN BALLOONS
Peter Guggi is probably the one that Hibs fans despise most but spare a thought for the Scandinavian who thought he was the dog's bollocks when he came to Easter Road. The name says it all - Thorsten Smugge.

TEAM TO HATE
A Hibs fan will stick anything in his veins and put anything in his mouth except Jam Tarts.

WORST RESULT OF THE 90's
Thumped 7-0 by Rangers at Ibrox.

CLUB COLOURS
Green, white, black, yellow, purple...anything the man at Umbro says they are.

1875 Hibs founded by Irish immigrants - thirteen years before Celtic. A fact that Hibs fans will bore you with frequently.

1888 Celtic founded. Hibs receive a letter from the SFA telling them they are no longer Scotland's major catholic club. Another letter arrives from Scotsport saying they no longer need the camera gantries as there's a cheaper option in Glasgow.

1903 Irvine Welsh's grandfather born in an opium den in Niddrie. Hibs win their first league championship. An event not to be repeated until the coming of "The Famous Five" - Dick, Julian, Anne, George and Timmy the Dog.

1950 The fifties were a halcyon period for the club. With the 'Famous Five' forward line they won league championships back-to-back in 50/51 and 51/52. They were also the first British club in European football. In 1955 they were invited to take part in the inaugural Champions Cup. They were beaten by Rheims in the semi-finals. *Record* headline - 'Reamed by Rheims'

1964 Heroin arrives in Britain. Hibs celebrate by beating Real Madrid 2-0 at Easter Rd when the legendary Jock Stein was their manager.

1968 The Summer of Love - and Edinburgh is flooded with top grade hash. Hibs are on a total high. They beat Napoli, (with the legendary Dino Zoff in goal) 5-0. This is the era of Hibee legends Stanton, Cormack and Marinello.

1982 Unreformed alcoholic George Best signs for Hibs. It was a partnership waiting to happen. He congratulates the club on their visionary training methods - cider and LSD.

1990 Wallace Mercer, owner of city rivals Hearts, stages a contro-versial attempt to take over Hibs and close them down. The 'Hands Off Hibs' campaign is born and the plan is defeated. Millionaire Tom Farmer - the 'Kwik-Fit Fitter' buys the club in 1991 from the receiver.

1998 Hibs are relegated to the First Division. Jim Duffy is replaced as manager by Alex McLeish. The 'Hands On Hibs' campaign is born. Pat Stanton stars in Channel 4 film *The Acid House* in which Hibs fan Happy Howden is buggered with a fake dildo.

1999 Hibs are runaway First Division champions and return to the top flight. Trinidadian star Russell Latapy arrives and is asked to play in the same midfield as Pat McGinlay.

1880
1890
1900
1910
20's
30's
40's
50's
60's
70's
80's
90's
2000

I fought the LAW

I t's one of the great anomalies of Scottish football that one of the country's most skilful and famous players was called Law - and that the vast majority of his fellow professionals have devoted their lives trying to break it.

Lawless footballers have done their damnedest to erode the fabric of our society so three cheers to *On The Ball* for keeping younger listeners informed about the evils and dangers of breaking the law. As social workers, probation officers and teachers abandoned their responsibilities in favour of smoking dope and listening to Gary Glitter records *On The Ball* stood up for common decency. Drink driving, common assault and vandalism are rife in our society and footballers are to blame. Some - like Celtic's Dutch winger Regi Blinker - have even gone to the extreme of peeing up a close.

In the following pages we reveal the vile lengths to which some footballers have gone in pursuit of criminal mayhem. *On The Ball* deplores their actions and begs young readers not to be influenced by their actions. Punching polismen is not funny so please don't do it. Scotland is a law-abiding country and if we don't protect ourselves from Kilmarnock's first team squad - who will?

If you see a footballer breaking the law ring the *On The Ball* criminal hotline on Saturdays on 0500 92 95 00. Our researchers are waiting for your calls - and remember, your information will be broadcast in the strictest confidence.

Chic Charnley

...he even managed to get sent off for punching one of his own team-mates as Dundee went down 7-2.

A S YOU'D EXPECT of someone who's had more send-offs than an entire armada of Clyde built ships, James 'Chic' Charnley also has first hand experience of the long arm of the law.

He has a shorter fuse than a suicide bomb and has had more rushes of blood than a Viagra junkie. In short, not a man you'd want to cross swords with - although a well armed team of neds made a valiant attempt during a Charnley training session in Maryhill Park a few years back.

During his football career Chic was sent off seventeen times - surely an entry in the Guinness Book of Records. During his spell at Dundee he even managed to get sent off for punching one of his own team-mates as Dundee went down 7-2. At the time of his off-field brush with the law he was still playing at Dundee and was driving home, after a couple of jars, in a courtesy car given to him by the club. Police were first attracted by the sight of a rusty Ford Anglia travelling at over 10 gallons per mile before noticing that the back lights were out. The officers said in court that Chic looked unsteady on his feet - the poor guy probably wasn't used to the exertion of walking up and down in a straight line.

He was fined £500 and banned for four years. But Chico is no daft laddie - he's been around for so long that he was failing to fulfil his potential when Eoin Jess was still a schoolboy star. In 1997, when he was with Hibs, an excellent start to the season led to calls for him to be selected for the national team. Sadly, an Irish granny couldn't be found and he didn't play for Celtic, Rangers or in the English Premiership. In fact he's now turning out for Kirkintilloch Rob Roy.

Petty Crimes #1   Derek Ferguson

IT'S HARD TO BELIEVE NOW but once upon a time Derek was the nation's favourite Ferguson brother. But as with so many internationalists at Ibrox it all went pear-shaped. He was shipped off to Tynecastle then ended up at Sunderland where, in 1993, he managed to cause a head-on collision by driving the wrong way round a roundabout at high speed. Always a keen proponent of an integrated transport policy, Ferguson criticised the design of the roundabout, claiming that it didn't conform with Department of Transport regulations. The judge pointed out that we drive on the left hand side of the road here.

Fined £2,300, banned for a year and sent to Falkirk.

Petty Crimes #2 Tom Callaghan

IT HAS BECOME STANDARD FOR SCOTTISH FOOTBALLERS to fall foul of the burdz - but Ross County midfielder Tom Callaghan's 15 minutes of infamy was the result of a badly behaved shihtzu called Charlie. After dropping off his air-hostess wife at Glasgow Airport Tom drove off with the little shihtzu leaping all over him. He was stopped for erratic driving despite his plea that his wife always had to say goodbye to the dog at the airport. Tom now has the distinction of being the first man since Hugh Grant to be arrested in a car with a dog in his lap.

Fined and quarantined for six months.

Petty Crimes #3 Regi Blinker

FANS - BUT CELTIC FANS PARTICULARLY - were shocked by the reports. Regi Blinker, streaming down the middle, spraying it left then right before finishing with a flourish and sticking it away. But this was no football game. This was in Queen Street in the early hours of a Sunday morning and Regi was proving that he could retain possession of the contents of his bladder about as long as he could a ball. Much to his embarrassment he was arrested and taken to the local nick where one of the officers said "When news of this gets back to wee Fergus you'll be out on urea."

Cautioned and sent to wash his hands.

biff

ouch

dinnae

Duncan Ferguson

B Y THE TIME HE WAS JAILED IN 1995 for assault on the pitch he was no stranger to the darker side of life. He'd already assaulted an off-duty police officer, gone for a guy on crutches… and played a handful of games for Glasgow Rangers. It was the latter that seemed to cause the greatest controversy - particularly after a British record transfer fee of £4m was squandered on him.

'Drunken' Duncan is infamous for being involved in one of the most shameful and criminal episodes in our entire footballing history - Estonia 0 Scotland 0.

His day of reckoning was at Ibrox Stadium in a match against Raith Rovers. A touchline incident between Ferguson and Raith's John McStay was closely followed by the best header of Big Dunc's entire Rangers career. Strangely, he wasn't red carded for the headbutt but swift police attention raised the prickly question of the law getting involved with football - something Donald Findlay QC would later make a song and dance about. As Dunc was on probation at the time of the offence he was later sentenced to three months in Barlinnie.

He hated life on the inside - cleaning, scrubbing, digging eight hours a day for £34.20 a week. It was just like being back at Tannadice. Still, big Jim McLean lifted his spirits when he wrote to say he wouldn't be visiting him - and he wasn't in long enough to miss an Everton win bonus. He found it hard to adjust to life back at Everton after his stretch. In the first match at Goodison he came off at half time and pissed in the trainer's bucket. He still can't get into the back of a black cab without putting a blanket over his head…and he said he didn't want to play for Scotland again as, after Barlinnie, he was terrified of the thought of being in the showers with another squad of Scotsmen.

Actually, his declaration just before the '98 World Cup that he was never going to play for his country again led to a tidal wave of uncontrollable apathy. He also said that when Scotland were kicking off against Brazil in the Stade de France he'd be on his honeymoon - probably the best chance he'd ever have of scoring during an international fixture.

Petty Crimes #4 Steve Kirk

STEVIE KIRK WAS A BIT OF A MISFIT during the Tommy McLean era at Motherwell. An attacking midfielder who regularly scored goals, he was never going to get a starting place so earned the nickname 'Supersub.' The frustration of defensive football eventually got to him and one day, in a fit of pique, he belted the ball up into the stand. Unfortunately it hit a young female supporter causing her to require hospital treatment. Steve got pelters. It was the first time since the Cantona kung fu incident that the shit had hit the fan.

Fined £250 and sent to East Fife.

Tam's Take...

It's 1996 and Mad Cow Disease is ravaging the countryside. Just outside Kilmarnock an Ayrshire bull leans over the fence and says "Bring on Kaiserslautern." Meanwhile the BSE crisis affects crowds further south at Somerset Park as the public heeds government warnings to steer clear of mince. Little do the fans know that before the crisis is over Killie will sign Ian Durrant and Ally McCoist. The transfer of two Ibrox legends means that Kilmarnock FC are mentioned in the football pages for the first time since 1929 when the Express interviewed 'S' form signing Ray Montgomerie.

Personally I still haven't forgiven Kilmarnock for the shabby way they treated Montgomerie in his testimonial year. Okay, they gave him a match in his honour, a sports dinner and a golf tournament - but why did they let him go to Partick Thistle? Mind you, Monty can always say he played in the same Killie team as Durrant and McCoist.

What can you say about Durrant? I'll never forget the night his son was born and he burst into tears when the midwife told him the baby was exactly 8 pounds. He only had a fiver on him.

Ally McCoist has never been short of dough. He may have been struggling though if Kilmarnock only paid appearance money as Coisty was always on the set of the Hollywood movie The Cup. Director Robert Duvall insists this is the most realistic football film ever made - sure enough McCoist's character fails to show up for Kilnockie's big match because he's too busy making a film.

Pat Nevin almost manages to out-jump the diminutive Kirsty Wark.

Stereotype FANS

IT'S DIFFICULT to find a suitable stereotype for Killie fans. They seem to wash, they have no significant contagious diseases and avoid religion. An *On the Ball* contributor claimed they are agoraphobics - they can't stand Ayr.

◦GARY HOLT with Cup.

CELEBRITY FANS

Cartoonist Malky McCormick. When they qualified for Europe, he bought a roll of blue and white towelling from a toilet supply company and had it made into a Killie suit. Also the *grande dame* of *Newsnight,* Kirsty Wark. She once told a magazine that her greatest embarrassment in life was her husband - a Rangers fan.

Bringing **Tommy Burns** into football management and refusing to let **Ally McCoist** retire with dignity.

"You can still see PARKHEAD from here Billy."

Kilma

'Kentucky Fried Chickens'

FASHION DISASTER

Dylan Kerr borrowed his first name from Bob Dylan, his second name from Jim Kerr and his hair-cut from Bryan Adams. When manager Bobby Williamson signed him the club were in Dire Straits

FORMER 'GER

Durrant, McCoist and Bobby Williamson were all team-mates at Ibrox. But only Williamson burnt his season ticket.

CELTIC DAFT PLAYERS

Mark Reilly is reputedly Celtic daft - and if that isn't sad enough never forget his nickname came straight from Coronation Street - 'Mavis' Reilly.

BIGGEST DUD

Ally McCoist - against Rangers - and Derek Anderson, who they successfully off-loaded on luckless Ayr United.

UNLUCKY SCOT

Defender Kevin McGowne made a brief claim for a Scotland cap in 1998 and in years to come will have to tell his grand-children that he was kept out of the Scotland team by Colin Calderwood.

BOSMAN BALLOONS

A true story. *On the Ball's* Stuart Cosgrove was flying to London to do his day job at Channel 4. Killie keeper Dragoje Lekovic was behind him with his family. When the plane arrived at Heathrow, Drago reached up in the luggage bins for a 40 ouncer of Vodka wrapped in a poly bag. The bottle slipped through Drago's hands and crashed on his son's head.

WORST RESULT OF THE 90's

Arch rivals Ayr United beat them twice in the Scottish Cup, three-nil and two-nil. Now that Glenbuck Cherrypickers have disbanded it doesn't get much worse than that.

FAVOURITE MEDIA CLICHÉ

Kilmarnock will forever be known as the winners of the "Family Final," which is a media euphemism for a big game unpolluted by sectarian bigotry.

GREATEST SCANDAL

Celtic steal manager Tommy Burns - and pay £100,000 fine after a tribunal. But that was a storm in a teacup compared to the public outcry when David Bagan was beaten in the heats of Mastermind.

FAVOURITE EXCUSE

Successive Kilmarnock managers like to blame the state of the pitch - any pitch.

COMMENTATORS NIGHTMARE

Christophe Cocard.

TEAM TO HATE

The one they have to share the county with - but when Ally McCoist and Ian Durrant were spotted on the terraces supporting their former club Rangers it gave Killie fans another reason to hate the Huns.

CLUB SONG

That old Ayrshire anthem - 'Walking in a Butlin's Wonderland.'

CLUB COLOURS

Blue and **White** - which confuses the elderly Ally McCoist. Killie are the ones in the stripes Ally.

...only Williamson burnt his season ticket...

'nock

Paul Wright
proving he can pat his head and rub something else at the same time.

MEN IN BLACK

Nobody in their right mind would want to be a referee in Scottish football but fortunately security at Carstairs has been lax over the last ten years and their has been a steady supply of applicants for the most thankless job in the world. Forget being a manager at Agnews in Jeddah - being a ref is the loneliest, most despised and truly dangerous job imaginable.

These are the rules. You spend years running up and down rain-soaked pitches in some god-forsaken hole in Ayrshire. The players are borderline psychopaths. Their beer bellies hang over their shorts and some of the tackles are so late that Virgin trains get there first. If you manage to avoid being mowed down by a minibus in Cumnock then maybe, just maybe, someone on the referee's committee will one day spot your talent.

So the big time awaits. You're promoted to running the line in a midweek game at Ochilview. You won't get home until midnight and the money on offer would be knocked back by a sweatshop worker in the Far East. But it's another step on the way to Nirvana - being a Grade One ref in the SPL.

On The Ball has always had a soft spot for refs. No one is quite sure why. Maybe it's because Tam Cowan's best mate Jim Walker was a ref before he injured his leg. Maybe it's sympathy for the oppressed…or maybe it's because there is no drearier experience than listening to phone-in shows where people whinge incessantly about some offside decision at a game you were nowhere near and couldn't possibly have seen.

That said there is much fun to be had at the expense of referees. Any fan who has travelled to an away match will have heard the term 'homer'. It's not the guy from the Simpsons or even the Greek philosopher. It's the bloke in the black shirt trying to endear himself to the home support by giving penalties that never were or booking your keeper for no apparent reason.

If the ref is not a 'homer' he is almost certainly a mason. This is one of the great enduring myths of Scottish football. FIFA may think that a referee is defined by a whistle, a notebook and red and yellow cards…but in Scotland it's a goat, trousers at half mast and a funny handshake. For conspiracy theorists and Celtic fans this will never change - Kennedy was shot by the CIA, Elvis is still alive and Rangers will get a penalty at Ibrox - especially in the dying minutes if the score is level.

Loved by none and hated by many, *On The Ball* pays a special tribute to the Men In Black.

Hugh Dallas

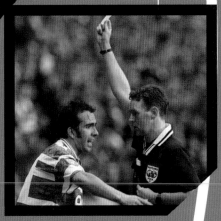

No matter what Hugh Dallas does in later life his name will always be synonymous with the phrase 'Old Firm Game of Shame.' The May '99 title decider at Celtic Park started quietly enough until a very ugly incident (are there any other kind?) involving Stephan Mahe resulted in the Frenchman being given the red card. All hell broke loose thereafter with bookings galore, pitch invasions, a Celtic fan diving head first from the stand "on his way for a pie" and - of course - the obligatory Rangers penalty. The most shocking incident came when Dallas, who was standing near the home support, was hit on the head by a pound coin. Blood was drawn and an official *On The Ball* enquiry was set in motion - just how did a Celtic supporter get that kind of money? A few weeks later Dallas was back in the thick of the action at Hampden for an Old Firm cup final amid the kind of security that would make Diana Ross nervous. The game itself passed virtually without incident and Dallas did not need the services of a double glazier on this occasion.

Dallas denies applying for the vacant general manager's job at Parkhead. But when the rumour was at its height there was a detectable shift of opinion among the Celtic faithful who were unanimous in saying "Bring back Jock Brown - all is forgiven."

Les Mottram

Les Mottram was responsible for one of the most bizarre incidents ever to take place on a Scottish football pitch when, in 1993, he failed to spot Dundee United's Paddy Connolly score a perfectly good goal at Firhill. To be fair, the United fans themselves had their doubts as they'd been waiting 8 years to see Connolly score a goal. But it gets weirder. If it wasn't a goal then the fact that Thistle's Martin Clark picked up the ball as it came back out of the net would have merited a penalty at least! But no, FIFA listed Mottram awarded a goal kick. The blunder was well covered by the media since, being at Firhill, half of the crowd were employees of BBC Scotland. To this day Paddy Connolly expects Jeremy Beadle to walk up him in the Gorbals and say "You've Been Framed."

Mottram was rewarded with a trip to the World Cup finals in the USA and enjoyed refereeing the South Korea v Bolivia match. In fact he enjoyed it so much he wished it would never end and it very nearly didn't thanks to almost 20 minutes of injury time.

After he retired in 1997 he signed up for a 'kiss and tell' exclusive and controversially accused all professional players of being cheats. He claimed that when he was out on the pitch it was 22 players against him. Except when the game was at Ibrox - then it was only 11.

Kenny Clark

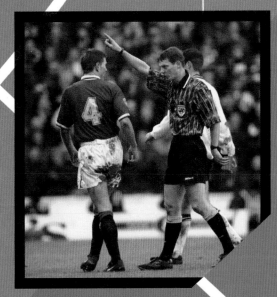

Although television pictures are not admissible evidence of innocence or guilt according to the SFA the Scottish media have other ideas - especially where Rangers are involved. Poor Kenny Clark has borne the brunt of two such decisions in his career.

The first involved the nation's favourite South African and all round soccer untouchable Richard Gough. When he scythed down Hearts' winger Neil McCann in a 1998 league game Clark sent him packing - much to the annoyance of the great man and to Walter Smith. The tackle has been shown on television more often than The Wizard of Oz and with more angles than a 3D tetrahedron.

The second occasion was in February '99. In a tense Motherwell v Celtic game following the Andy Goram 'basement of bigotry' brouhaha, Clark managed to send off practically the only Catholic on the field - John Spencer. Spencer tried to show what a true Brit he was by giving a two fingered salute to the Irishmen in the crowd - a detail the unsighted Clark missed completely. An honest mistake? Or has he just become too used to Rangers players giving dodgy handshakes? In another controversy last season he missed Henrik Larsson's gestures to St. Johnstone fans after a Celtic defeat at McDiarmid. However, the incident was reported by one of the refereeing assistants - or Tayside Police as they're more commonly known - enabling Clark to pass on the details to the SFA.

John Rowbotham

John Rowbotham has suffered for his profession. He has the most predictable string of nicknames in the game - Kojak, Uncle Fester, Right Said Fred etc. His bald pate has singled him out for cruel abuse and the poor guy must lie awake of a Saturday night with the chorus of "Hair, Hair, He's No Hair" ringing in his ears.

Rowbotham will be forever remembered as the first person in Scotland to send Paul Gascoigne packing - or second if you count Gazza's ex-wife Sheryl. The momentous event happened during an Old Firm match in November '97. Rowbotham had lost his day job a couple of days earlier and after being given his cards he was obviously keen to try them out. So when Gascoigne was involved in a minor skirmish with Celtic's Morten Wieghorst he was sent off for possibly the most weak-hearted attempt at the Dane since Papworth Hospital's production of Hamlet. Cynics suggested that he was making up for a previous blunder -not sending the fat Geordie off two years previously when he'd clearly head-butted Aberdeen's John Inglis in the chest during a game at Ibrox. That had been an incident so screamingly unmissable that even the Scotsport camera crew managed to capture it on film. Rowbotham was officially downgraded after that clanger.

In September '99 he was involved in further controversy. At half time in a Motherwell v Hearts match with the home side 1-0 up he called the game off because of a waterlogged pitch. The Motherwell players were outraged - particularly club captain Andy Goram who has never been known to be put off by a wet patch near the box.

Willie Young

After giving Paul Gascoigne yellow card number nine-in-a-row in 1996 Willie Young incurred the wrath of Gers boss Walter Smith. Walter accused referees of picking on the loveable Geordie scamp - a player who used his elbows to greater effect than Nigel Kennedy. But Smith complained that the treatment handed out by Young and others would make overseas stars think twice about coming to play in Scotland. Of course, Rangers have always shown warm hospitality towards their foreign visitors…AEK Athens, Strasbourg, Juventus…

Willie Young was honoured to be in charge of the 1998 Cup Final between Hearts and Rangers played at Celtic Park. With Rangers having lost out in the League and in the League Cup this was their final chance to rescue a potentially barren season. Things got off to a dramatic start when Young awarded a penalty to Hearts in the first minute following a foul on Stevie Fulton. Cameron made no mistake with it and Adam doubled the damage at the start of the second half.

In the last minute, with Rangers 2-1 down, the ageing chat show host Ally McCoist fell over in the general vicinity of the penalty box. All the years of training and the nights at the Lodge fell by the wayside as Willie immediately awarded a free kick instead of a penalty. Young had done the unthinkable. A referee was right! But only the once.

MEN IN BLACK

Competitions

2

IN WHAT PROVED TO BE THEIR WORST EVER START TO A SEASON, beleaguered Aberdeen cheered up *On The Ball* by signing a new keeper from Darlington. His name was DAVID PREECE. Surely Aberdeen Chairman Stewart Milne knew the consequences of signing a keeper whose name rhymed with fleece. *On The Ball* invited limericks with the opening line "An Aberdeen Goalie called Preece..."
Here are the top answers:

An Aberdeen Goalie called Preece...

Was coached by the great Cyd Charisse
A dancer she was
And that's fitting because
Dons defend like the chorus from *Grease*

(John Samson, Edinburgh)

An Aberdeen Goalie called Preece...

Was arrested by Grampian Police
For fiddling with sheep
And for groping Bo Peep
So he fled and now lives in Dumfries

(Stuart Murdoch)

An Aberdeen Goalie called Preece...

Had fingers covered in grease
So thanks to his arsin'
Viduka and Larsson
Said "Cheers mate!" and grabbed two apiece

(David Tonner, Motherwell)

An Aberdeen Goalie called Preece...

Was caught as he played with his piece
Five against Celtic
Was really pathetic
But he'd coated his fingers in grease.

(Drew Malarkey, Glasgow)

An Aberdeen Goalie called Preece...

Was famed from Dundee to Dumfries
Bit in Aberdeen it's true
The fans don't have a clue
If he's full time or only on lease

(Tom Meikle)

An Aberdeen Goalie called Preece...

Was lifted by Northern Police
Was told what he'd done
He'd smiled at a Hun
And here that's a breach of the peace!

(Yes, it's Steve Letford from Oban again!)

An Aberdeen Goalie called Preece...

Has sexual relations with geese
He then tried an otter,
moved onto its' daughter
And now he's been nabbed by Police.

(David McLennan, Pitlochry)

Stereotype FANS

Taxi drivers, redundant steel workers and general shirkers.

Mother

'the UB40's'

Stuart Says...

WHO CAN FORGET that scene from *Deliverance* in which ugly misfits and vile inbreeds hunt a group of visitors from the city. Most people imagine it was filmed on location in America's deep South…but it was actually shot in Motherwell.

Spotting a Motherwell fan is not easy these days - and for readers who have never been in a red-neck bar it can be an upsetting experience. The first step is to get them to talk about their school days. You'll know the one with the cross-eyes is a Motherwell fan if he went to Braidhurst High School and was in the same year as his dad. A Motherwell fan will always talk excitedly about his school days, especially Third Year - the happiest five years of his life.

What about women fans? Ask the lady in the corner by the one armed bandit (but be careful not to be too curious - he lost it in an accident at the meat packing factory.) If she's been on the Jerry Springer Show more than twice there's a good chance she's a Motherwell fan. To be totally sure get her to talk about her love life. If she thinks safe sex is a pink padded headboard then it's a safe bet she has a season ticket for the Davie Cooper Stand.

And what about the kids? Well you could always talk to the wee boy with the runny nose and the 'jeely-jar' glasses. His school friends run around the playground with ntl: on their strips but he is happier wearing the claret and amber polo neck his Granny knitted him for Christmas. Poor wee soul, sitting outside the pub waiting on his babysitter, he must be a Motherwell fan. That's five hours he's been there reading the label on a bottle of orange juice. Mind you, it did say 'concentrate'.

CELEBRITY FANS

PANTO STAR and social club legend CHRISTIAN, now starring in *Puss In Boots* at Motherwell Civic Centre. Also NEIL REID, who rose to fame when he sang *Mother of Mine* on Opportunity Knocks in 1974 and TAM COWAN who didn't.

Greatest Contribution to On the Ball

THEY SIGNED **ANDY GORAM** and his photo album. Also the fact that it's the only club in the UK where the Chief Executive not only turns out for the team but also happens to be the manager's brother in-law.

CELTIC DAFT

OWEN COYLE, the player who is the tabloid's favourite green grape. He moved to Dunfermline and has still to play for the only team he ever wanted to play for. He was replaced by Chief Exec. Pat Nevin - the thinking man's Celt.

Owen Coyle auditions for *Riverdance*.

Post-Kamp men.

*Well

...they decide to accept milk tokens as admission...

FASHION DISASTER
Goalkeepers -Sieb Dykstra's moustache or Andy Goram's teeth.

FORMER 'GER
Billy Davies, John Spencer, Andy Goram etc…almost enough for a marching band.

BIGGEST DUD
Eddie May, who was bought from Falkirk for Steve Kirk, Paul McGrillen and £100,000. What a bargain - for Falkirk.

BOSMAN BALLOONS
Former manager Harri Kampmann who specialised in players who wouldn't have cost a penny even before the Bosman ruling.

TEAM TO HATE
It used to be Hamilton Accies before they became a roving band of football gypsies. Now 'Well supporters can sympathetically patronise them.

WORST RESULT OF THE 90's
Beaten by Alloa in the League Cup…but worse than that, beaten 6-5 by Aberdeen at Fir Park in October 1999.

FAVOURITE MEDIA CLICHÉ
"Holiday Tycoon John Boyle"

GREATEST SCANDAL
See 'Biggest Dud.'

FAVOURITE EXCUSE
The vast number of buses that leave Motherwell for Ibrox and Parkhead.

COMMENTATORS NIGHTMARE
Eliphas Shivute. Although his name was tricky to pronounce it was a tabloid writer's dream. Close enough to Elvis for dire headlines and a poor family back home to patronise.

CLUB SONG
'(I don't want to go to) Wishaw.'

CLUB COLOURS
Buckfast and **Lager.**

JOHN BOYLE leads first team training.

---

history

1886 Motherwell formed from an amalgamation of two local metalworks teams and are admitted to the Scottish League's new 2nd Division in 1893.

1895-96 Move to Fir Park. In the first game of the season 6,000 fans turn up to see them reamed 8-1 by Celtic. Much the same as today really.

1912-13 Motherwell turn out in the 'claret and amber' racing colours of Lord Hamilton of Dalzell for the first time.

1926-27 The start of Motherwell's most prolonged period of success. For the next seven years they finish in the top three, eventually winning the League championship for the only time in their history in season 1931-32. Then they succumb to the Great Slump (that's not the worldwide Depression - just the normal Lanarkshire one.)

1950-51 Motherwell win League Cup, beating Hibs 3-0 in the final. The following season they lift the Scottish Cup…beating Dundee 4-0.

1970's In the early years of the decade Motherwell compete in the Texaco Cup - the tournament for British clubs who couldn't qualify for Europe. They record victories over Stoke and 'Spurs. The dole queues begin to lengthen in Lanarkshire

1983-84 Motherwell relegated to 1st Division. The dole queues lengthen further. In a bid to attract more support the club offer concessions to anyone who *doesn't* have a UB40.

1984-85 Tommy McLean appointed manager. In a snub to Thatcher, Motherwell bounce back and win promotion to the Premier. In a further snub they decide to accept milk tokens as admission.

1991 Motherwell win Scottish Cup - 4 -3 over Dundee United in memorable match. Ally Maxwell has such a great match in goal for Motherwell that Rangers feel obliged to sign him.

1994 McLean resigns. Alex McLeish takes over as manager and when he moves on to Hibs in season '97-98 his replacement is Harri Kampmann.

1998-99 Another kamp man - millionaire package tour operator John Boyle - becomes club Chairman. Installs Billy Davies as manager, Pat Nevin as Chief Exec… and Andy Goram as captain. What a team.

1890
1900
1910
20's
30's
40's
50's
60's
70's
80's
90's
2000

OFF THE BALL

Off The Ball's acronym competitions are amongst the most popular and produce some answers which are creative genius or just plain weird!

FRANK McAVENNIE

Failed **R**estaurateur **A**nd **N**ookie **K**ing **M**ight **C**ock **A**n **E**xtended **N**ostril **N**ervously **I**n **E**xplanation

(Stephen Boyd, Glasgow)

JIM FARRY

Job **I**s **M**eaningless. **F**at **A**dministrator's **R**emoval **R**equired **Y**esterday

(Graham Crawford, Glasgow)

BRIAN LAUDRUP

Bluenose **R**uns **I**n **A**nd **N**iftily **L**aunches **A**n **U**nconvincing **D**ive **R**esult - **U**njust **P**enalty

Dave. (You know who you are)

DONALD FINDLAY

Dour **O**range **N**arcissist **A**nd **L**awyer **D**enounces **F**enianism, **I**nspiring **N**ostalgic **D**iehard **L**oyalists **A**ll **Y**ear

(Graham Crawford, Glasgow)

CELTIC

Catholic **E**nclave **L**acks **T**rophies **I**n **C**upboard

(George Henry, Edinburgh)

STEPHANE MAHE

Scientists **T**ry **E**xplaining **P**henomenal **H**aircut **A**s **N**ightmare **E**xperiment. **M**asochism **A** **H**obby **E**vidently

(Stevie Robertson, Glasgow)

Competitions

3

PAUL GASCOIGNE

Persistent **A**lcoholism **U**nderlies **L**oathsome **G**luttony.
Always **S**trikes **C**heryl. **O**minously **I**nconsistent **G**azza **N**eeds **E**ngland
(Stephen Higgs, Neil MacLeod and James Annal, Dingwall)

WIM JANSEN

Where **I**s **M**anagerial **J**oker **A**ppearing **N**ow? **S**urely **E**astenders **N**igel!
(Ian MacDonald, Glasgow)

SANDY ROBERTSON

Sozzled **A**lthough **N**icely **D**ressed **Y**outh **R**apped **O**ld **B**ouncer.
Enjoyed **R**ide **T**o **S**aughton. **O**ut **N**ow.
(John Cairns, Perth)

STEWART MILNE

Sheep **T**hrilled - **E**specially **W**ith **A**djustable **R**ug - **T**herefore
Mutton **I**s **L**ately **N**ever **E**nding.
(J. Angus, Largs)

STUART COSGROVE

Sharp, **T**houghtful, **U**nbiased **A**nd **R**ichly **T**alented **C**onsistently **O**ffering
Supporters **G**enerous **R**ations **O**f **V**intage **E**ntertainment
(Ian McCleary, Kilmarnock) *(Crawler!-Ed)*
OR
Saints **T**umshie, **U**seless **A**t **R**adio **T**alk, **C**lothes **O**rdinary, **S**tupid **G**lasses.
Result? **O**verweight **V**eritable **E**ejit!
(Chris Reilly, Aberdeen)

TAM COWAN

Talking **A**bout **M**otherwell **C**auses **O**besity, **W**rinkles **A**nd **N**ausea.
(Ian McCleary, Kilmarnock)
AND
Tedious **A**mplified **M**otormouth **C**omes **O**n **W**ireless **A**nd **N**iggles
(W. Oliver, Grangemouth)

Tam's Take...

I HEAR PARTICK are about to clinch a sponsorshop deal with a sex shop. They're hoping to get a cream that will help them stay up. And Jim Oliver is looking to sign a one-eyed black lesbian saxophone player. But where in the West End of Glasgow would he find someone like that?

MANAGER JOHN LAMBIE is often criticised but it's great to know that he does his bit for Children in Need. Last year he made the ball boys at Firhill redundant. Let's hope the good times come back for the Jags though - who can forget 1992 when they reached the quarter finals of the Glasgow Cup?

As the **SAVE THE JAGS CAMPAIGN** continued Murdo McLeod pledged his support for the club by promising he'll never manage them again. Star of *Gregory's Girl* Dee Hepburn also offers to help the club. Thistle boss John McVeigh said he'll persevere with Gareth Evans for another month and get back to her.

SADLY Scotland's most loveable club folded in March 2001.

Greatest Contribution to On The Ball

THISTLE GOING BUST IS ALWAYS GOOD FOR A LAUGH... and of course John Lambie and his doos. He was once asked how he had inspired the team in the dressing room after a first half hammering and replied "Ah cried them a bunch o' poofs"

CELEBRITY FANS
The Krankies, Craig Ferguson, Dorothy Paul and a catalogue of 'B' list celebrities from the BBC Canteen.

Stereotype FANS

Media luvvies and Glaswegian dissenters who find sectarianism objectionable and who would rather discuss the Maryhill Magyars in a Byres Road wine bar.

CELTIC DAFT PLAYERS
CHIC CHARNLEY - the only team he ever really wanted to play for and he eventually did in a friendly against Man.Utd.

Partic

'Oliver's Army'

Charan Gill and 'Gorgeous George.'

GREATEST SCANDAL
"If anyone thinks we're going to give away a company which we've built up over six years at a personal loss to satisfy the wishes of some Indian with a curry shop they'd better get real." - Jim Oliver, referring to the takeover bid in 1995.

FAVOURITE MEDIA CLICHÉ
'Partick Thistle-Nil'

FAVOURITE EXCUSE
The base sectarian nature of the West of Scotland militates against the success of a forward-looking non-sectarian multicultural team such as Partick Thistle. And by the way - he's behind you.

COMMENTATORS NIGHTMARE
Icelandic dud Hreinn Hreingsson.

TEAM TO HATE
Both branches of the Old Firm …but don't rule out Maryhill Juniors when they're on a good run.

FASHION DISASTER
The famous cup winning team of 1971 pioneered perms and flares but even they would have baulked at Chic Charnley's powder blue zoot-suits.

FORMER 'GER
Nicky "what a shag" Walker and Colin Jackson were both former infidels.

UNLUCKY SCOT
Chic Charnley. If the game against Manchester United had been three years earlier he'd have been Scotland captain.

BOSMAN BALLOONS
Kamajl Advu - a Swedish born Kosovar from Bury - is a Bosman balloon par excellence. But connoisseurs of the 'dire import' will always have a soft spot for Hispanic haddie Jesus Tejero - he only managed one good cross.

WORST RESULT OF THE 90's
Most Thistle fans are so busy remembering Jackie Husband and the good old days that the dire performances of the '90's have failed to register.

BIGGEST DUDS
Murdo McLeod as manager.

CLUB SONG
Mary fae Maryhill.

CLUB COLOURS
Red, yellow and **black** - great for a packet of wine gums but as a football strip?!?

" …a socialist republic and vegetarian Bovril…"

THISTLE FC

Another great Jags goal sends the fans wild.

1876 Founded when a peformance of Cinderella at the Criterion theatre was cancelled. Their first recorded match was against 'Valencia' - not the Spanish outfit but another local junior side. At least Thistle managed to beat Valencia 1-0.

1909 Thistle move into Firhill after thirty years as Scottish football's original gypsies, playing in no less than six different grounds. The previous year they had almost gone out of business. So what's new.

1921 Thistle win Scottish Cup. Puss In Boots plays to sell out crowds at the Hippodrome.

1922 Record crowd at Firhill of almost 50,000 against Rangers. But a 500,000 crowd storms George Square demanding a socialist republic and vegetarian Bovril.

1948-49 Thistle's Willie Sharp scores fastest ever goal in the history of the Scottish League - in 7 seconds. But that's where the urgency ends - he's still waiting for his bonus.

1971-72 Thistle win League Cup beating Celtic's fading and over-rated "Lisbon Lions" 4 -1. Rikki Fulton says it's the happiest day of his life since he played Widow Twanky at the Citizens.

1975 Thistle miss out on a place in the new Premier League…but gain promotion the following year under new manager, over-rated 'Lisbon Lion' Bertie Auld.

1981 Thistle win Glasgow Cup. The organisers refuse to present the trophy as the rules clearly state the cup is reserved for Rangers or Celtic.

1988-89 John Lambie takes over as manager. Signs players such as Chic Charnley, Davie Elliot, Davie Irons, Jim Duffy, Buttons and Peter Pan. They win promotion to Premier League in 1992 and star in Aladdin at the Metropole.

1995-96 Murdo Mcleod takes over as manager. Thistle relegated to 1st Division but win Maryhill and District Shield. A takeover bid by a consortium of Asian businessmen led by Charan Gill and backed by local M.P. George Galloway fails when the club refuses to change its name to Paratha Thistle.

1997-98 Thistle relegated to 2nd Division but win Firhill Five a Side Complex Cup. Fans demand that new manager - Baron Hardup - is sacked.

1880 1890 1900 1910 20'S 30'S 40'S 50'S 60'S 70'S 80'S 90'S 2000

The Broons

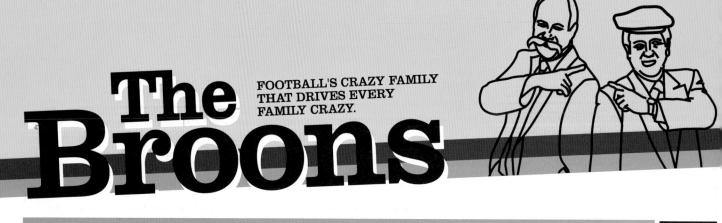

FOOTBALL'S CRAZY FAMILY THAT DRIVES EVERY FAMILY CRAZY.

JINGS, CRIVVENS AND HELP MA BOAB. Little did Ma and Pa Broon realise just how famous their bairns would become. It all began at 10 Dweeb Street, Hamilton. As a duo, Craig and Jock delighted family and friends with renditions of popular tunes of the day such as 'My Love is Like a Blue, Blue Nose' and 'Stop yer Ticklin' Jock.' Younger brother Jock loved to be the centre of attention and at the age of eight wrote a bitter diatribe against his primary school teacher who had the gall to criticise his numeracy skills by saying that he was not "arithmetic minded." As for Craig, he was always popular with primary school teachers.

As teenagers the pair continued their education at Hamilton Academy. Craig was controversial even then. When choosing sides for the playground kickabouts he would go for the only English lad in the class before the local scruffs. After leaving school he signed for his beloved Rangers in 1958 then transferred to the Tayside "bluenoses" - Dundee - in 1960. It was during his Dens days that he cut the world renowned skiffle records with the group called "Hammy And The Hamsters". Ma and Pa Broon were proud of their wee boy. Also around this time he auditioned - unsuccessfully - as a dancer on the BBC's *White Heather Club*. Undeterred he managed to get a gig on the STV equivalent *Jig Time*, presented by Jimmy Shand and Jim Delahunt.

MEANWHILE, Jock left the Academy to study Law at Cambridge. The rarified atmosphere of student life was a breath of fresh air for the Hamilton Academic. He captained the football team against Oxford to earn a sporting blue which has remained with him to this day. On leaving the ivory towers he wrote a harsh account of university life entitled 'Academic Minded', which convinced him he should pursue a career in journalism - then inexplicably joined DC Thomson.

BY THIS TIME Craig had carved out a career in education, specialising in primary school teaching. Appropriately, in 1966, he joined the Bairns and in the 70's became manager of "The Bully Wee".

THE BROTHERS' careers almost crossed when Jock was briefly Secretary to the Scottish League between '68 and '70. But after that he took up practice as a lawyer, specialising in sports law. His breakthrough in broadcasting came in 1980 when STV gave him the chance to share his greatest passion with the nation - the sound of his own voice. He managed to stick Scotsport for a whole ten years before trading himself to the BBC's Sportscene.

DURING THE 80'S Craig had become more and more involved with coaching Scotland and in 1986 was appointed Andy Roxburgh's assistant. After years of managing league no-hopers Clyde he was thrilled at the opportunity to be able to work with some Rangers players.

IT WAS FINALLY in 1993 that the Broon brothers became a double act again. After the fall of Roxburgh - the first manager for 24 years who didn't get us to the World Cup finals - Craig took over the helm as the national coach. His first task was an away game in Italy. His second was to answer some 'probing' questions from his wee brother at the post-match interview. Jock's questions were ferocious -
What is PC Murdoch's profession?
When is Granpaw's birthday?

THE SCENE WAS SET for a future of scintillating interviews but that was mercifully cut short by the appointment of Jock as general manager of Celtic in June 1997. Wee Fergus was hassled with contracts, transfers and press harrassment and needed somone to take care of the annoying details. So Jock resigned from the Beeb - but not before publishing his damning critique of sporting bias at BBC Scotland - 'Partick Minded.'

The Broons

FOOTBALL'S CRAZY FAMILY
THAT DRIVES EVERY
FAMILY CRAZY.

IT WAS DOWNHILL all the way for the new Celtic supremo. Jock quickly discovered that he could do no right in the eyes of the Celtic faithful who were deeply suspicious of his Cambridge Blue. But Jock tried to pacify his critics by saying that "As of now I am the biggest Celtic supporter in the country". Some weeks later Davie Hay was driven out of Parkhead for being too much of a Celtic traditionalist. It did not go down well with the supporters but then neither did Jock's failure to hold on to players such as Di Canio, Van Hooijdonk and Cadete or the apparent determination to drive out Championship winning manager Wim Jansen and his assistant Murdo McLeod.

NOT TO BE UPSTAGED on the controversy front big brother Craig set about redressing the balance. The nation was shocked by the newspaper headlines about Craig singing foul-mouthed sectarian songs to his girlfriend's answer-phone. No one could fathom an answer to the controversy - just how did a dumpy wee guy like him get a burd like that?!? Craig strenuously denied the accusations of bigotry, claiming that he would call his Celtic supporting girlfriend Phyllis Kirk before Linda Slaven, who had made the allegations. He also pointed out that *'Flower of Scotland'* could be construed as a nasty, xenophobic, nationalist song with anti-English sentiments and could be considered offensive by some people - half his current squad for example. Ultimately he was dumped - although he managed to hang on to his job.

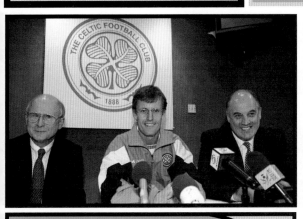

BUT IT WAS ALL OVER for Jock at Celtic. He couldn't handle the pressure of being the man who drew up Harald Brattbakk's contract any more… and when Fergus sent him to recruit a top new coach he came back with an old age pensioner. So Jock fell on his sword. In any case, he was tired of the Hurley - and the Burley - and yearned for a quiet life. He tried his hand at the arse end of a pantomime cow…but eventually settled for a place where people wouldn't pester him with phone calls and where he wouldn't have to be answerable to anyone. He was delighted to take up the offer of his own show on Scot FM. Don't call them - they call you.

OFF THE BALL

In November 1997 *Off The Ball* asked for suggestions for the **shortest football book in the world**. Some of the best answers were:

The 1997 Guide European City Guide - **by Walter Smith**
(David Allen, Aberdeen)

A Great Night Out In Perth - **by Stuart Cosgrove**
(Jonny Walker, Glasgow)

The Partick Thistle Cheque Book
(Alan Gardiner, Glasgow)

Easy Steps to Discreet Hair Dyeing - **by Roy Aitken**
(Derek Boyle, West Lothian)

Knee Injuries And How To Spot Them - **by The Ibrox Medical Staff**
(Ed McDonald, Glasgow)

The Charlie Nicholas Guide to the Queens English
(Alan Gardiner, Glasgow)

...AND one year later we asked for **football's shortest videos**...this is what the fans suggested...

Tommy McLean - **The Raith Rovers Days**
(Archie Nicol, Skelmorlie)

McCoist and MacAulay - **The Funny Bits**
(Ed Webster, Aberdeen)

St Johnstone - **Meet The Fans**
(Neil Davison, Dunfermline)

Harald Brattbakk's Greatest Goals
(Bruce McGuiness, Kilmarnock)

Motherwell FC's Great Foreign Signings
(Alan Henderson, Kirkcaldy)

Donald Findlay Sings Daniel O'Donnell
(Colin Dowie, Bridge of Don)

Competitions

4

IN OCTOBER '99 - on hearing the news that Seb Rozenthal was apparently about to make a comeback at Ibrox - we asked fans for their own particular views on this phenomenon and it tapped a rich vein of creative genius...we were overwhelmed.
Those that follow were the best of about 300 entries.
ROZY - YOU NEVER KNEW YOU WERE SO POPULAR!

Seb Rozenthal's coming back soon

It's the main talkin' point in the toon
But the twist in the tale
Is he's no longer male
He's had a sex change and now he's called June
(Willie Reid)

Seb Rozenthal's coming back soon

It's a while since he's been aroon'
When he was last here,
The cost of a beer
Was two groats and half a doubloon
(Colin Wright, Glasgow)

Seb Rozenthal's coming back soon

He still looks like a blonde Daphne Broon
His problems have meant
That Rangers have spent
More than NASA to put man on the Moon
(David Crombie, Buckie)

Seb Rozenthal's coming back soon

His health has been up and doon
There'll be a big roll of drums
When he finally comes
Wrinkled and old, like a prune.
(Bill Ferguson, Cardross)

Seb Rozenthal's coming back soon

And the Tartan Army love Craig Broon
Ian Ferguson's no' dim
And the refs are a' Tims
And the Dons are no' goin' doon!
(Stephen Dines, Balloch)

Seb Rozenthal's coming back soon

He'll be here by the last day of June
E.T. will appear,
Gazza will give up the beer
And the cow will jump over the moon
(Colin McGowan, Glasgow)

Seb Rozenthal's coming back soon

The size of a hot air balloon
His mammoth weight gain
Has put strain on the 'plane
Cause it took off from Chile last June!
(Tiger Hamilton, Dunfermline)

...MORE ROZY LIMERICKS ON PAGE 94!

The Chairman of Fife Regional Health Board takes in the big game.

Stereotype FANS

LINO CUTTERS - or as the Habitat catalogue prefers to call them - Marmoleum Technicians.

Raith

'the Geordie Munros'

Greatest Contribution to On The Ball

WINNING THE LEAGUE CUP in '95, allowing *On The Ball* to get it so far up Celtic it hurt…but don't forget the day 'Drunken' Duncan Ferguson head-butted Raith full-back John McStay. (See *I Fought The Law.*) This led to one of the show's greatest long running sketches - 'Duncan's Prison Diaries' which won Tam Cowan a Sony award for anal innuendo.

Tam's Take…

Gordon Brown may be their celebrity fan but this is not where their political connections end. Did you know that David Blunkett is currently the Chief Scout at Stark's Park?

When Jimmy Nicholl announced he was leaving the club to join Millwall the Raith fans gathered outside the ground with knives, pick-axes and baseball bats. They weren't demonstrating against the Rovers board - they simply wanted Nicholl to know what he was letting himself in for by moving to The Den.

Raith almost succeeded in signing former porn star Moses Njbuda. Apparently the scouts first clocked him performing superbly in one of his videos called Moses and The Burning Bush. A porn star would of course look the part in any line up and it was rumoured that Moses could shoot well from a long distance although he did most of his best work inside the box.

Sadly Moses didn't sign. He was keen on a move but the club couldn't agree terms with his llama.

He's off to jail and you're off to Albion Rovers.

history

1880
1890
1900
1910
20's
30's
40's
50's
60's
70's
80's
90's
2000

FORMER 'GER
Kirkwood was a former 'Ger but Jimmy Nicholl was always there to upstage him when the Daily Ranger came calling to ask "Tell us Jimmy, how much are you missing Ibrox?"

GREATEST SCANDAL
Tommy McLean's tenure as manager must have been the shortest in the history of Scottish football before he was poached by Dundee Utd.

OVERS

CLUB SONG
Unfortunately the club song is the subject of litigation between Raith and the Idaho Tourist Authority.

...succeeded in signing former porn star Moses Njbuda...

FAVOURITE MEDIA CLICHÉ
"They'll be dancing in the streets of Raith."

FAVOURITE EXCUSE
We're only a provincial team.

COMMENTATORS NIGHTMARE
If it's a Channel 5 commentator forget players with weird names - they can't even pronounce Kirkcaldy.

FASHION DISASTER
Stevie Crawford - his girlfriend was a hairdresser and she used to expirement on his head.

CELTIC DAFT
Shaun Dennis couldn't wait to get a green shirt on his back. But even with Malky McKay in their back four Celtic didn't want him. So he signed for Hibs.

BIGGEST DUD
Jim McInally or Dave Bowman. The moral of the story - never sign pensioners from Jim McLean.

UNLUCKY SCOT
Gordon Dalziel was unlucky to be born with the biggest hooter in Scotland. Fearing an adverse reaction from FIFA, Craig Brown never picked him. The same rule did not apply to Tommy Gemmell. Mind you, he played for Celtic.

BOSMAN BALLOONS
Odd Arald...and no, it's not a reference to Celtic's alleged striker Brattbakk. Sadly, Odd only played for one half of a game against Dunfermline. So *On The Ball's* favourite Raith Balloon is trialist Moses Njbuda - the former Swedish porn star.

TEAM TO HATE
Dunfermline. Also Falkirk - which must go back to the 2-1 defeat the Bairns inflicted on Raith in the Scottish Cup Final of 1912 -13. More recently Raith took a dislike to Cockney club Millwall, selling them six rank players and a manager.

WORST RESULT OF THE 90's
Beaten by Arbroath in the Cup. For those of you who doubt the credibility of that the publishers insisted we repeat it...beaten by Arbroath in the Cup.

CLUB COLOURS
Any shade that looks nice when it's fitted to your lobby.

AWAY

1883 Founded by a bunch of delivery boys who were sacked for refusing to carry rolls of lino under their arms. They claimed it meant walking through Kirkcaldy like Dick Emery.

1891 Raith move to Stark's Park which, to this day, is the only Scottish ground that is a rhyming couplet.

1902 The carpet is invented. Kirkcaldy is thrown into economic gloom. To cheer them up Raith are admitted to the Scottish League.

1933 The Raith team become the only team in Britain ever to be shipwrecked! This happened near Gran Canaria while Rovers were on a pre-season friendly tour. Neither Celtic nor Rangers have ever matched this achievement although in Europe they have often sunk without trace.

1948-49 Raith are runners up in the League Cup and are promoted to the First Division where they remain anonymously until relegation in 1963.

1992-93 Raith hit the big time under manager Jimmy Nicholl - they are promoted to Premier as 1st Division Champion. Dougie Donnelly gets gig to advertise Sterling Carpets in Tillicoultry near Stirling. Lino sales shoot up. Raith are back!

1994-95 Victors over Celtic (on penalties) in League Cup Final. Undoubtedly the highlight of the club's history. As a token of respect Chick Young mentions them twice in one programme. Techno dominates the charts but SFA refuse request to change their name to Rave Rovers. Barry Lavety breaks off signing talks and goes to Hibs instead.

1995 Raith take on the might of Bayern Munich in the UEFA cup - played at Easter Road. Bayern's Jean-Pierre Papin was seen warming up behind one of the goals. Undaunted by the sight of one of the world's great players a Raith supporter resplendent in Parka and bunnet rose from his seat and yelled "Papin - you're shite!"

1997 The glory days are over - Raith are relegated to the 1st. Jean-Pierre Papin watches Sportscene from his Paris apartment and shouts "No' as shite as you are Dargo!"

1998-99 Jimmy Nicholl's second coming as manager comes - and goes - as Raith struggle to stay in the 1st Division.

Website-1

Do you remember Saturday 31st July 1999? Yes, it was the day before Aberdeen stormed off on their dismal run. But it was also the day when *Off The Ball* launched its very own web site - clearly flouting the BBC's public service broadcasting remit to "educate, entertain and inform"...

EVERY WEEK we encourage footie fan surfers to provide witticisms to attach to the tempting images featured in our 'Frame Game' competition. The attractive pictures of Tam Cowan came from BBC Choice Scotland's *Offside* programme. HERE'S SOME OF THE WINNING CAPTIONS SO FAR...

⇨ "Look, it worked for Gail Porter, and I'll get the best one projected on to the Scottish Parliament building."
(Sheila Letford)

⇨ "Don't kid yerself, Rhona - that's no' a microphone in ma pocket."
(Duncan Hay)

⇨ "Do you think I'm the new Des Lynam?"
(Alan McLean)

⇨ "Saints fans enjoy a rare moment of European success in Finland with local Lapp dancer, pictured left, Maka Minesaheineken."
(Malcolm McCandless)

⇨ "A draw for the Saints and I've got a lumber. What a night!"
(Steve Letford)

⇨ "Look lads, it's that crap guy from Channel 4 - Harry Hill."
(Alan Raeburn)

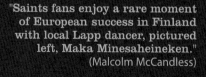

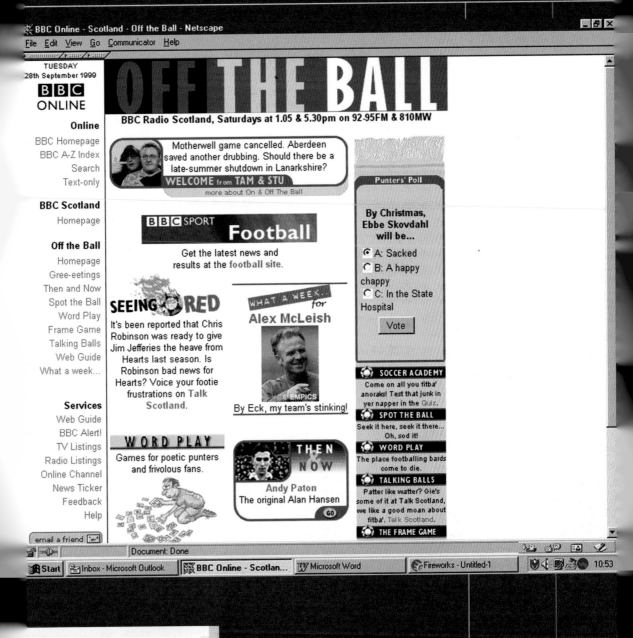

www.bbc.co.uk/offtheball

BBC Online - Scotland - Off the Ball - Netscape

File Edit View Go Communicator Help

TUESDAY
28th September 1999

BBC ONLINE

Online

BBC Homepage
BBC A-Z Index
Search
Text-only

BBC Scotland

Homepage

Off the Ball

Homepage
Gree-eetings
Then and Now
Spot the Ball
Word Play
Frame Game
Talking Balls
Web Guide
What a week...

Services

Web Guide
BBC Alert!
TV Listings
Radio Listings
Online Channel
News Ticker
Feedback
Help

email a friend

OFF THE BALL

BBC Radio Scotland, Saturdays at 1.05 & 5.30pm on 92-95FM & 810MW

Motherwell game cancelled. Aberdeen saved another drubbing. Should there be a late-summer shutdown in Lanarkshire?
WELCOME from TAM & STU
more about On & Off The Ball

BBC SPORT Football
Get the latest news and results at the **football** site.

SEEING RED
It's been reported that Chris Robinson was ready to give Jim Jefferies the heave from Hearts last season. Is Robinson bad news for Hearts? Voice your footie frustrations on **Talk Scotland**.

WHAT A WEEK for Alex McLeish
© EMPICS
By Eck, my team's stinking!

WORD PLAY
Games for poetic punters and frivolous fans.

THEN NOW
Andy Paton
The original Alan Hansen
GO

Punters' Poll

By Christmas, Ebbe Skovdahl will be...
○ A: Sacked
○ B: A happy chappy
○ C: In the State Hospital
[Vote]

SOCCER ACADEMY
Come on all you fitba' anoraks! Test that junk in yer napper in the Quiz.

SPOT THE BALL
Seek it here, seek it there... Oh, sod it!

WORD PLAY
The place footballing bards come to die.

TALKING BALLS
Patter like watter? Gie's some of it at Talk Scotland, we like a good moan about fitba'. Talk Scotland.

THE FRAME GAME

Document: Done

Start | Inbox - Microsoft Outlook | BBC Online - Scotlan... | Microsoft Word | Fireworks - Untitled-1 | 10:53

⇨ "Yes, I know who the father is - it's Derek Johnstone."
(James Bain)

⇨ "Am tellin' ye, wan o' them Aliens is gonnae burst oot any minute. Honest!"
(Brian Madden)

⇨ "Eh-oh! Tinky Winky eat all Tubbycustard."
(Barry Craig)

X

Glasgow Rangers

Ibrox: The Tradesman's Entrance.

'Chick's Eleven'

Tam's Take...

IT WOULDN'T BE WISE for me to say anything against the current squad as I've no wish to be accused of being anti-Catholic. But seriously, I hear Donald Findlay shaved off his moustache and slipped into the ground claiming he was Daniel Prodan - which worked a treat as no-one knows what Prodan looks like.

It's nonsense to suggest that Rangers were founded in 1690 - real die-hards know it was 1986 when Graeme Souness took over. Also, where would they be without David Murray? He planned a 'Rangers Radio' station. It was to be a bit like Radio Clyde but with less about Rangers. The music would be from the 1960's and the 1690's. Murray himself was tipped to be the stations first shock jock - he would go on air and announce the prices he's charging for the Ibrox car park.

Murray also announced plans for a Disney style theme park called Hunderwest World. It's believed the carousel will have white horses only. Gordan Petric and Seb Rozenthal were offered short term contracts to work on the ghost train. Talking about crocked players, we shouldn't forget to pay tribute to the Rangers doctor - the quack who once gave Stephen Hawking a clean bill of health.

Greatest Contribution to Football

A CATALOGUE OF CHAOS and scandal has follow-followed Rangers over the years. Durrant's kebab, Gazza's flute, Duncan's doos, Andy's armband and the sash Donald Findlay's father wore. But beyond all the rituals of bigotry, drunkenness and sectarianism…they did give Scottish football **Mrs Jardel.**

Stereotype FANS

Plumbers from Peterhead who think it's good for their business and broadcasters from Glasgow who claim to be St Mirren fans.

Dick Advocaat before

Dick Advocaat after

CLUB SONG
'Theme from Scotsport'

THE DRESSING ROOM FROM HELL
Goram, McCoist, Durrant and Gazza

CLUB COLOURS
Red, white, blue, yellow, beige, aquamarine, powder pink, violet, turquoise. Yes, who can forget Mark Hateley's jackets.

FAVOURITE MEDIA CLICHÉ
Rangers *are* the media's favourite cliché.

FAVOURITE EXCUSE
It was a private function!

COMMENTATORS NIGHTMARE
A goal against Rangers.

FASHION DISASTER
Gazza's bad hair days as Blondie and Blackhead ...and then of course Dick's hairweave.

TEAM TO HATE
Where have you been since the league began?

FORMER 'GER
See biggest dud. Also see Hearts.

GREATEST SCANDAL
A three way tie between Gazza at Gleneagles, Andy Goram in a caravan and Donald Findlay in a home video. But connoisseurs of scandal will remember Jim White trying to emulate Jeremy Paxman when he interrogated Brian Laudrup on Scotsport. The first question was the tough one : "Brian, why are you so good?"

CELTIC DAFT PLAYERS
Mo Johnston was Rangers' first high profile genuflector. Now most of the team cross themselves when they run on to the pitch… but the only current player who has admitted he's a bit of a Celtic fan on the side is Giovanni van Bronckhorst who sneaks into Parkhead to watch his old pal Henrik Larsson.

BIGGEST DUD
In a team of millionaires, Craig Moore is the rich man's Gregor Stevens. They bought him, sold him and - amazingly - bought him again.

UNLUCKY SCOT
You're joking. Anyone who pulls on a Rangers jersey gets a complimentary game for Scotland. But even the SFA selection committee choked on their tomato soup when Rangers insisted Ally Dawson got a cap.

WORST RESULT IN THE 90's
Hiring Hannibal Lecter as team doctor.

CELEBRITY FANS
Oasis boss Alan McGhee. That's their only claim to pop fame now that Andy Cameron has left The Chemical Brothers. Other media fans include Johnny Watson, Jim White and celebrity chef Gordon Ramsay who played for Rangers reserves in the 70's when Ibrox was the home of the orange soufflé.

BOSMAN BALLOONS
Oleg Salenko, Erik Bo Andersen and Peter Van Vossen are hard to upstage. But the man who has dared to challenge them is the Russian Mafia's favourite fall guy Alexei Kanchelskis.

Dick advocate - always

HISTORY

1870

1880

1872 Founded on the South side of Glasgow - a date disputed by many historians who think it was actually 1690. The name Rangers was inspired by an English rugby team. Pity it wasn't Harlequins.

1891-92 Rangers share the inaugural Scottish League championship with Dumbarton. The Daily Record fails to mention Dumbarton.

1890

1902 Moved to the site of the present Ibrox Stadium, the capacity of which is 51,000. That's 1,000 locals plus 50,000 arriving in buses from Inverness, Aberdeen, Dumfries etc.

1900

1911 An emergency meeting of Lanarkshire referees is convened in secret as Rangers complete nine years in a row without winning the championship.

1920 The Legendary Bill Struth is appointed manager. A strict disciplinarian, Struth fines a Rangers youth team player for feeling up a Suffragette outside local night spot *Queen Victoria's*.

1910

1954-55 Bill Struth is still manager. In his 34 years he won 18 of Rangers' total of 48 League Championships and 10 of their 28 Scottish Cups. But the old dud never won the Tennents Sixes.

20's

1967 Rangers beaten 1-0 in the Scottish Cup by Berwick. Former paratrooper and war veteran Jock Wallace is in goal for Berwick. He celebrates with his team mates and is surely still hungover a few years later when he agrees to become Rangers manager and signs Gordon Smith.

30's

1972 Rangers find success in Europe by beating Moscow Dynamo 3-2 in the final of the Cup Winners Cup at the Nou Camp in Barcelona. Clashes between fans and police afterwards led to a one season ban for Rangers so they became one of the few clubs never to get the opportunity to defend the trophy.

40's

50's

1986 Graeme Souness becomes manager and signs some really big names…like Michailichenko. His most controversial signing though is Maurice Johnston -the former Partick Thistle and Watford striker. Rangers die-hards rip up their season tickets outside Ibrox. Football fans throughout the world wonder what they have against Partick Thistle and Watford.

60's

1994 Rangers are bounced out of the European Champions League by AEK Athens. By coincidence a supporter's club in Carfin is immediately renamed the Demis Roussos branch. A week later Rangers are beaten by Falkirk in the Coca-Cola Cup. But no-one names a bus after Campbell Christie.

70's

1998 Dick Advocaat, star of international hairweave adverts, takes over as Rangers manager. With the Campbell brothers already installed at Dunfermline *On The Ball* is disappointed that he is not the first Dick to manage a Scottish premier side. But is he the first boss to share his name with a Christmas cocktail?

80's

90's

2000

OFF THE BALL

Off The Ball prides itself on the literary talent it has helped unearth over the years. Who else gives a voice to Scottish football's disaffected - not the Record Hotline, that's for sure! At half-time in fine stadia across the nation, soccer scribes nibble on macaroon bars and jot down limericks, anagrams and acronyms referring, sadly, to players' chances of..."scoring".

Website-2

Here are some of the recent offerings to our weekly acronym section...

⇒ **"Derek Johnstone"**

Durable **E**rection **R**egularly **E**xtends **K**in. **J**iffys **O**rdinarily **H**elp **N**egate **S**exual **T**ransgressions, **O**bstructing **N**ewborn **E**ditions
(David McLaughlin)

⇒ **"Andy Goram"**

Any **N**ubile **D**amsel **Y**earning **G**reatly **O**f **R**omance, **A**void **M**idden
(Thomas Robertson)

⇒ **"Aberdeen"**

Always **B**uying **E**very **R**otten **D**iddy, **E**bbe **E**xits **N**ext
(Graham King)

t he Off The Ball website limericks are also popular with ex-pat punters and others overseas with an interest in the Scottish game. Here's a recent example all the way from Oz....

To the big squad wee Burchy's been brought
making Pa Broon extremely distraught
For he can't sing The Sash
for the dressing room bash
So the words wee Burchy needs taught
(Danny O'Brien, University of Sydney, **NSW, Australia**)

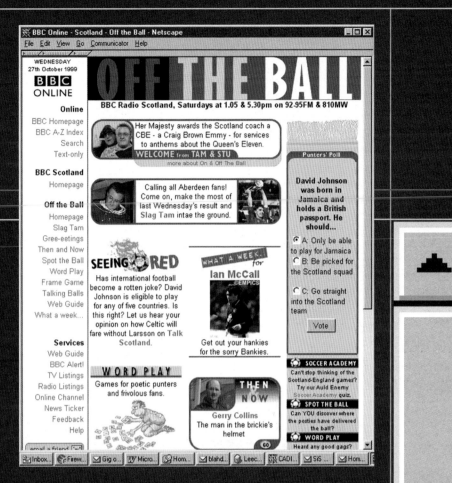

The site also acts as a place where jokes come to die.
Interestingly, they tend to be sent in by fans who have
no sense of comic timing or intonation but who
nevertheless feel they can **write** a joke if not tell one.

A SUNDAY LEAGUE TEAM is desperate for players. So desperate in fact that one Sunday they are forced to play a chicken. Rather surprisingly the chicken has a brilliant first half. One minute it's clearing off its own line, the next threading the perfect through ball, the next putting in a perfect cross. At half time all its team-mates are very pleased and everyone runs back onto the pitch for the second half. On the way the ref starts chatting with the chicken.
"Great first half, mate. You must be really fit."
"Thanks," replied the chicken, "I try to keep myself fit, but it's difficult finding the time so I try to do an hour in the gym each morning before work."
"What do you do then?" asked the ref.
"I'm a chartered accountant," replies the chicken.
At which point the ref immediately brandishes the red card and sends the chicken off.
The bemused team-mates gather round the ref and start complaining.
"Sorry lads", says the ref, "I had no choice. Professional fowl."

(Bob Hay)

A BLOKE IS HAVING A QUIET DRINK IN A BAR, leans over to the big guy next to him and says: "Do you wanna hear a Rangers joke?" The big guy replies: "Well, mate, before you tell that joke, you should know something. I'm six-feet tall, 15 stone and I am a season ticket holder at Ibrox. The guy sitting next to me is 6'2", weighs 17 stone and is a member of a flute band. Next to him is a bloke who's 6'5", weighs 20 stone and he's a current grand master of the Orange Order. Now, do you STILL want to tell that Rangers joke?" The first bloke says: "Nah, not if I'm going to have to explain it three times."

(Gerry McArdle)

So there you have it, a taster of the old tat that's on
the Web. Why not check out the real deal on
www.bbc.co.uk/offtheball. It almost
makes it worth getting sacked from your job for
Internet abuse.

ST JOHNSTONE FANS get a look at their latest signing.

St. JOH

'the Wurzels'

Tam's Take...

I WOULD NEVER knowingly upset St Johnstone fans - as they're five of the nicest guys I know. So I'll just congratulate them for their sterling contribution to Scottish football.

After all, who can forget the Scottish Cup semi-final against Rangers in 1998-99, when Parkhead catering staff reported a whopping £13.60p passing through the till. It would have been even less but the Saints fans were absolutely starving as they had just come off the back of the worst harvest in living memory.

I was happy to congratulate them on qualifying for Europe and I know how excited they must have been flying out to Finland. Surely, the first time most of them had been in a plane without spraying the crops.

Incidentally, did you know that Saints fans from the infamous 'Hunters' housing scheme don't mind being called tractor drivers. It's the only time they'll get anywhere near a good change of gear.

Greatest Contribution to On The Ball

St Johnstone's legendary tea lady AGGIE MOFFAT once banjoed Graeme Souness and became a regular *On the Ball* character ever since. Aggie once boosted the team's morale by taking them on a night out to the bingo - it was the only time the McDiarmid Park players witnessed a full house.

Stereotype FANS

AGRARIAN PEASANTS who still vote Tory and drive tractors.

CELEBRITY FANS

FILM STAR **Ewan MacGregor,** comedian **Fred MacAulay,** and the boy with the big ears from **Taggart** .
What's the connection between Fred MacAulay and Kilmarnock?
They both had to team up with **Ally McCoist** to get publicity!

STONE

> ...he preferred to work in his father's fish shop...

FASHION DISASTER
Andy Rhodes' jerseys and Nic Dasovic's hair. Dazza had to give up a career as a guitarist in the Canadian thrash metal band The Virgin Whores. He briefly tried to re-form the band in Perth but couldn't find any virgins.

FORMER 'GER
Gary Bollan. The hypocritical Stuart Cosgrove once called him a dud on live radio. He now refers to him as the legendary BoBo. What will he say when Derek McInnes agrees terms?

CELTIC DAFT PLAYERS
A three-way fight between John O' Neil, Paddy Connolly and 'Pope' John-Paul McBride.

BIGGEST DUD
Euan Donaldson. After being humped by Stenhousemuir, Saints boss Paul Sturrock paid £80,000 for the Stenny full back - and then freed him. New club Clyde thought he was still over-priced.

UNLUCKY SCOT
Alan 'Jesus' Main. He's prone to spectacular blunders but that has never ruled anyone out of playing in goal for Scotland. Sadly for Main he's Scottish - and that has.

BOSMAN BALLOONS
Striker **Lars Gunnar Karstrand** turned down Saints because he didn't want his rottweiller to go into quarantine. Another Swede, **Peter Norren**, said he preferred to work in his father's fish shop. Saints fans were gutted.

TEAM TO HATE
Definitely **DUNDEE**. In a bitter last day of the 1961-62 season, champions Dundee relegated Saints. The Dee are nicknamed **the 'coagies'**- Perth slang for the filthiest members of a tinker family.

FAVOURITE MEDIA CLICHÉ
"A well run family club."

GREATEST SCANDAL
The media think it was Alex Totten's sacking, but Saints fans were infinitely more upset when he was replaced by John McClelland.

FAVOURITE EXCUSE
Hayfever. Too much grass in Perthshire.

COMMENTATORS NIGHTMARE
Attila Sekerlioglu getting a goal... or complaining about the half-time cuppa when Aggie's in ear-shot.

WORST RESULT OF THE 90's
Stenhousemuir beat them 5-0 in the League Cup. Saints slumped even further when they lost the only final they were ever expected to win - the B&Q Challenge Cup. Danny Griffin put the ball in his own net and Stranraer paraded the silverware round town in an open top ferry.

CLUB COLOURS
Royal Blue and **White**. The colours once confused the teenage **Ally McCoist** who thought he'd agreed to sign for Rangers.

CLUB SONG
'I've Got A Brand New Combine Harvester'

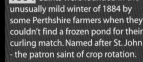

1884 Saints were founded in the unusually mild winter of 1884 by some Perthshire farmers when they couldn't find a frozen pond for their curling match. Named after St. John - the patron saint of crop rotation.

1924 Saints decamp to Muirton Park and leave their original pitch - the Old Recreation Grounds on Perth's South Inch. The club's original stadium is now a toilet frequented by latter day George Michael fans.

1936 Three shepherds witness a miracle when Roddy Grant is born in a manger. Sadly, they can't find three wise men in Bathgate. The shepherds came bearing gifts - gold, frankincense and twenty Embassy Regal.

1944 Geoff Brown's dad wins contract to build air-raid shelters in Crieff. Saints win Best in Breed at Perth Agricultural Show.

1964 Miguel Simao's mum wins a ticket to see The Four Tops in Lisbon. Saints win WRI Shield for best home-made tablet.

1971 Saints most famous team features Henry Hall and John Connolly. In the League Cup final against Celtic, Hall was clean through on the keeper and certain to score when his famous comb-over hair-cut became entangled in his boot.

1978 Ally McLeod's Scotland squad requires players to have perms. No St Johnstone players go to Argentina as this trend didn't reach Perth until 1992.

1988 The ground that Henry Hall once graced is sold to ASDA who pay tribute to the club with a special St Johnstone check-out for ten fans or less.

1999 Third place in SPL wins Saints a coveted place in the UEFA cup. The fans travel to Monte Carlo singing 'In your Monaco Slums'. The last time Perth fans marched into Europe, Vera Lynn was singing 'White Cliffs of Dover'.

1884
1890
1900
1910
20's
30's
40's
50's
60's
70's
80's
90's
2000

Competitions

5

...MORE ROZY LIMERICKS CONTINUED FROM PAGE 83...

Seb Rozenthal's coming back soon,

To excite our leader Craig Broon
Cause we know where he'll be -
Checking Seb's family tree
To see if he has a granny fae Troon
(John Smart, Dundee)

Seb Rozenthal's coming back soon,

Robson's signed Cosgrove for the 'Toon
Tam Cowan is slim
Iain Ferguson's a Tim
And the Dons will be champions come June
(Chris Brookmyre, Aberdeen)

Seb Rozenthal's coming back soon,

They say it's the talk o' the toon
For he's bought an abode
Way down the Ayr Road
Cause he's heard that it's Chile in Troon
(Iain MacDonald, Orkney)

Seb Rozenthal's coming back soon,

Folk say he's been to the moon
The last time he played
There was a German air-raid
And the Japanese advanced on Rangoon!
(Robert Reid, Inverurie)

Seb Rozenthal's coming back soon,

Scotland's sexiest man is Craig Broon
Aberdeen were delighted
to beat Man United
Aye...an' Donald Findlay turned Catholic in June!
(Ian Dalziel, Troon)

Seb Rozenthal's coming back soon,

He'll be joining the Rangers platoon
Though one leg's in plaster
It's no' a disaster
The other's on wheels and goes roon'
(George Waddell, Glasgow)

Seb Rozenthal's coming back soon,

But this time it's 'Last Chance Saloon'
If he doesn't strike gold
for the Huns, he'll be sold
And will find himself wearing maroon!
(Francis and Linda, Barra)

Seb Rozenthal's coming back soon,

He's been out longer than 'Dark Side of The Moon'
Last time he was a 'Ger
Chick Young still had hair
And the Yanks still had subs at Dunoon.
(Derek England, Bishopton)

STUART on Tam

I first met Tam Cowan ten minutes before we went into the studio to record the first episode of *On the Ball*. I would like to pretend it was a memorable moment and the beginning of a long and dear friendship. But why lie?

Tam Cowan is as obnoxious as he is fat. He proudly boasts that his favourite comedian is Bernard Manning, his favourite singer is Engelbert Humperdinck and his favourite media personality is Roger Melly – the man from the Telly.

Put simply Cowan is a dinosaur - a throwback to a forgotten era in Scottish evolution when men kept pigeons and Motherwell won matches. I have never met anyone who is so suspicious of progress or so contemptuous of anyone from outside Lanarkshire. This is a man who thinks that sending e-mail is a sign of homosexuality.

A few months ago in August, I took a break from the cultural rigours of the Edinburgh Festival and went for a walk in the St James' Centre. It was a fortunate coincidence; a local branch of RS McColl's had a copy of the tenth anniversary of the Hearts fanzine *No Idle Talk*.

On the back of the fanzine was a photograph used to promote *On the Ball*. It is not a flattering photograph - I could lose a few pounds - but by comparison Cowan is what his hero Roger Melly would describe as a salad-dodger, the male equivalent of a Fat Slag.

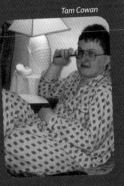

Tam Cowan

Tam Cowan has never endeared himself to Hearts fans and I was delighted to see they were using their fanzine to retaliate. The winning caption accompanying the photo was written in the style of an advert putting Tam Cowan up for adoption through Greater Glasgow Health Board. The Hearts fans fondly described him as "radio's answer to John Merrick."

The BBC have tried to persuade me to abide by the normal rules of the media and say how honoured I am to work with Tam and congratulate him for the charity work he does for children with leukaemia. But it would be a callous fraud.

Every Saturday night when the show is finished he leaves the BBC studios and heads directly for Shawfield Stadium to gamble license-payers' money on the fate of greyhounds. It is always a forlorn night. By midnight he is virtually penniless and barely has enough money left to pay the poor waiters at the Taj Mahal restaurant in Glasgow, who are forced to stay late and listen to his painful patter.

By 1 o'clock Cowan is thankfully tucked up in his bed at home, snoring and farting like a beached whale, and dreaming of the day when Motherwell get an away point at Perth.

Dream on fatso.

TAM on Stuart

Stuart Cosgrove was born in the small farming village of Perth in 1925. Always a fierce patriot, the 14 year old took the king's shilling in September 1939 after convincing the local army recruiting officer he was 16.

He's been lying about his age ever since. Without wishing to embarrass the man, Cosgrove remembers when Heinz had only one variety. And - not a lot of people know this - his passport picture was done by Rembrandt.

Stuart is easily the most famous St. Johnstone fan in the country. Mind you, when you consider the numbers we're talking about that's a bit like saying Dr. No is Ursula Andress's best known motion picture.

I've often accused the Channel Four boss of being a total media poof but it's only fair to point out that - thanks to his dubious past as a 'hard man' soccer casual - he always insists on drinking his Bacardi Breezers straight from the bottle.

At a time when most of his peers are quite content to slip into the old demob suit for a night out, Stuart continues to cut about the perfumed bars of Glasgow in his 'trendy' combat trousers. Honestly readers, it's like catching Dame Thora Hird in a pair of pedal-pushers and a peephole bra.

Stuart Cosgrove

Fans of Cosgrove's outlandish gear will undoubtedly recall the ridiculous white hooded top he wore while appearing on Scotsport last season. Looking like Cadfael the mediaeval detective after a rough night on the absinthe, the old pro sailed through the show and was dead chuffed when host Jim Delahunt remarked "That's honestly the most horrendous item of clothing that's featured on this programme since Arthur Montford hung up his sportsjackets. Two minutes later an irate Mr Montford called STV and left the following message - "My arse!"

But enough harsh words. Stuart often describes yours truly, his trusty sidekick, as "a fat lump of Lanarkshire lard." But deep down I know he likes me. In fact - and I hope this doesn't make him blush - he treats me like the grandson he never had.

Following the release of *Hampden Babylon* the *On The Ball* Annual is Cosgrove's second football publication that's destined for the 50p basket in Bargain Books.

Time to hang up the quill Pops.

The **ON THE BALL** Annual was written by Stuart Cosgrove and Tam Cowan with additional material by Stephen Hollywood, Angus Lyon, Andy Scott and Ian Turner.

Researchers: Paul Bradley, James Evans, Jim Mason.

For their help thanks go to: Sean Allan, Sandra Brown, Paul Bundy, Rab Christie, Gill Davies, Alistair Devine, Paul Gilfillan, Robin Grimmond, Paul Hutton, Jim Jackson, Tony Law, John Millar, Keir Murray, Dougie Reid, John Thomson and Steve White.

Images supplied by Mirror Syndication International *(unless otherwise stated)*

Editor: Angus Lyon   Executive Editor: Neil Fraser.